Information and Communication Technology
for Intermediate GNVQ

GW00600714

2nd edition

Information and Communication Technology

for Intermediate GNVQ

W.W. Milner & Ann Montgomery-Smith

stanley thornes GNVQ

First published in 1997 by:
Stanley Thornes (Publishers) Ltd
Delta Place
27 Bath Road
CHELTENHAM
GL53 7TH
United Kingdom

Second edition published 2000

00 01 02 03 04 / 10 9 8 7 6 5 4 3 2

A catalogue record for this book is available from the British Library

ISBN 0 7487 5315 X

Line illustrations by Angela Lumley; cartoons by Shaun Williams

Typeset by Florence Production Ltd, Stoodleigh, Devon
Printed and bound in Spain by Graficas Estella S.A.

Contents

Acknowledgements

The authors and publisher gratefully acknowledge the help of Colin Jones, who provided useful comments on the manuscript throughout the writing process.

Photo credits

- Gateway – page 115
- Hewlett-Packard Ltd – page 120
- Intel Corporation (UK) Ltd – page 121
- Matrox (UK) Ltd. – page 122
- Quickshot (Europe) Ltd. – page 117 (bottom)
- Tony Stone Images – page 154
- Trip/H. Rogers – page 117 (top)

Dedication

This book is dedicated to the IT students at Joseph Chamberlain College.

Induction to the course

What is covered in this unit

0.1 **What is a GNVQ?**

0.2 **Intermediate GNVQ in Information and Communication Technology**

0.3 **Key Skills**

0.4 **Course assessment**

0.5 **Working on your own**

At the end of the induction you will be asked to provide a newsletter or wall display which can be used to describe this course to interested parties. This will explain the course content, how it is taught, how it is assessed and how you are expected to work. It will also introduce members of the course team. You will also have made some notes about your own working practices and some skills that you may find helpful.

Materials you will need to complete this unit:

You will need access to the hardware and software that you will use during the course. This should include at least:

- a word processor
- an art package
- desktop publishing facilities
- a spreadsheet
- a database
- access to the Internet
- printers.

Introduction

You have chosen to study for an Intermediate Level GNVQ in Information and Communication Technology. This course usually takes one academic year to complete and you will be assessed on the work that you complete during the course. This introduction allows you to make sure that this is the right course for you, and to help you to complete it successfully.

A GNVQ course will be different in many ways from general school courses.

- It is an introduction to working in information technology.
- You will be expected to behave as an adult and can expect to be treated as an adult, with the respect and responsibilities.
- Having been given a 'work task' or assignment to produce you will be responsible for producing the work on time.
- It is your job to produce and keep evidence of work done.
- All the work on the course involves information technology.

Information technology students at Joseph Chamberlain College, Birmingham

0.1 What is a GNVQ?

GNVQ stands for General National Vocational Qualification. A **vocational** qualification is one aimed at a particular type of work. In your case, for work in information technology (IT). It is a general qualification in that it is not specific to a particular type of work in information technology and can be useful for a number of different jobs or further study.

Vocational is a term used about work in a particular type of trade or profession.

Employers have been involved in designing GNVQ courses, and have been asked what skills and knowledge they require of workers in IT. What you learn on this course will be useful to you when you look for work in IT. The skills and knowledge are split into Units, three of which are mandatory: Using IT to Present Information, Using IT to Handle Information, and Understanding IT Hardware and Software. You will also study three optional units selected from the range offered by your awarding body/educational establishment. You are likely to be offered the opportunity to complete work for a **Key Skills** qualification, the three key areas of which are Communication, Application of Number and Information Technology.

What types of skills do employers require of the workforce in addition to vocational skills?

Key Skills are Skills required by employers from all their workers, in addition to their vocational skills.

Activity 1

Make notes about the units that you will be studying.

a Name each unit.
b Write down five specific points on what you expect to learn from each unit.
c What materials will you need for each unit?
d Who will tutor the unit and when and where will they tutor you?
e How much work will you be expected to do on your own?

0.2 Intermediate GNVQ in Information and Communication Technology

GNVQ in Information Technology is a course about using **PC**s at work. It is not about computer games, not even educational ones. It is about using and understanding computer **hardware** and **software** for business purposes. You will learn to understand and use **operating systems**, **application packages** and **computer communications** in IT.

JARGON DRAGON

A *PC* – which stands for 'personal computer' – is a small computer which can be used on its own for a large number of uses. It can also be networked to other computers. Most people think of a PC when they think of a computer. Large expensive computers which were shared by all computer users in an organisation were invented before small cheap ones. In the 1980s computers became small enough and, more importantly, cheap enough for personal use. This was the start of information technology as we know it today.

The *hardware* is the machines, gadgets and wiring making up a computer system.

The *software* is the programs used by the computer system.

The program running the computer hardware is known as the *operating system*. A computer cannot work without an operating system and an operating system is not needed without a computer. Examples of operating systems are Windows, MS-DOS and MacOS.

An *application package* is a program that makes a computer do a particular job. Application software copies, and often improves on, what is otherwise done without a computer. Examples are Word, Paintbrush, Excel.

Computer communications allows computers to connect with each other. Examples of use are e-mail, Internet.

Most people use only a very small part of the power of their computers. They learn to use a few options only of any computer program, and never get round to finding out what else it can do. This is so common that IT professionals have invented a name for them – the 80/20 club. They say 80% of computer users only ever use 20% of the possible facilities of any computer application package.

If you recognise yourself as a member of the 80/20 club, then this course is not for you. You will be expected to explore any package you use to the full, and be able to use most of the facilities. Ask yourself these questions:

1 Do I like to try a new computer package?
2 Do I explore the menus and find what they can do?
3 Do I like to find quicker ways of doing something on the computer?
4 Do I use help screens if I can't find how to do something?
5 Do I show my friends new tricks with the computer?
6 Do I like solving problems?

7 Do I keep trying if something doesn't work first time?
8 Do I like to try things out for myself rather than wait
    to be shown?
9 Do I like to make things work?
10 Do I enjoy using computers?

If you answered *yes* to most of these questions you will probably succeed in this course. If you answered *no* to more than four questions or to question 10 you might like to discuss with your tutor whether you are on the right course.

/ **Activity 2** /

a Name three computer programs that you have used and enjoyed. State two things you liked about each.
b Name one computer program that you have used and did not like. State one thing that you disliked about it.

/ **Activity 3** /

Work in pairs or in a group of three.

a Find out from your partner/s:
   • Their name.
   • What computer hardware and software they own, have use of at home, have used before.
   • What they like best about IT.
   • What IT magazines they like to read.
   • What they hope this course will lead to.
   • Something about them that makes them stand out from the crowd.
b Using an appropriate computer package, write a newspaper article about your partner/s, including one or more headlines and a graphic image. The articles can go on a wall display or in a newsletter to introduce the students on the course to each other.

Where does the course lead?

Jobs in IT can be divided into three types.

Jobs using IT

Most jobs in IT are of this type. They include jobs in offices, in business, in art and design, retail, banking, automation, leisure and accounting. Most jobs nowadays use IT and an intermediate GNVQ in IT will help you in any trainee job at this level.

Supporting IT users

With so many people using IT as part of their work, people are needed to help them use the systems. Work in this area includes system support as a technician or running a help desk.

A technician at work

A technician's work includes making sure that the equipment is working correctly, that printers have paper and ink, that faults are corrected, that users are advised of new hardware and software. Trainee technician work is sometimes available at intermediate level.

Running a help desk involves sorting user problems as they arise. It involves learning the technology very thoroughly and getting on well with people.

Many firms recruit at a higher level than intermediate GNVQ for support staff, but may move junior staff from other areas to this type of job if they show aptitude.

Developing IT systems

This involves setting up a system to do a specific job. The system is developed using a suitable application program such as a spreadsheet, database, system design tool or even a programming language. There are very few jobs available in systems development at intermediate level. Most firms recruit trainees at advanced level or direct from universities.

Further education

An Intermediate GNVQ in Information and Communication Technology can lead to:

- an Advanced GNVQ in ICT
- most other Advanced GNVQ courses
- some A-level courses.

After Advanced GNVQ or A-level, students can go on to university in appropriate subject areas.

0.3 Key Skills

Key Skills are an important part of GNVQ study. The main three Key Skills are Communication, Application of Number and Information Technology – although you can also study in the areas of Working with Others, Problem Solving and Improving Own Learning and Performance. You will have the opportunity to provide evidence of Key Skills when completing activities in this textbook. In order to obtain a GNVQ qualification you will need to achieve Key Skills as well as a pass in your IT units.

Communication

You will need to demonstrate that you can do the following.

C2.1a: Contribute to a discussion about a straightforward subject. You will have provided evidence that you can:

- make clear and relevant contributions in a way that suits your purpose and situation
- listen and respond appropriately to what others say
- help to move the discussion forward.

C2.1b: Give a short talk about a straightforward subject, using an image. You will have provided evidence that you can:

- speak clearly in a way that suits your subject, purpose and situation
- keep to the subject
- structure your talk to help listeners follow what you are saying
- use an image to clearly illustrate your main points.

C2.2: Read and summarise information from *two* extended documents about a straightforward subject. One of the documents should include at least *one* image. You will have provided evidence that you can:

- select and read relevant materials
- identify accurately the lines of reasoning and main points from text and images
- summarise the information to suit your purpose.

C2.3: Write *two* different types of document about straightforward subjects. One piece of writing should be an extended document and include at least *one* image. You will have provided evidence that you can:

- present relevant information in an appropriate form
- use a structure and style of writing to suit your purpose
- ensure that text is legible and that spelling, punctuation and grammar are accurate, so your meaning is clear.

'That seems to summarise the manuals nicely!'

Remember – Communication Skills

- Move discussions forward.
- Give a short talk using an image to illustrate your main points.
- Read and summarise information from extended documents.
- Use a suitable structure and style when writing extended documents.

Activity 4

Work in a group of 3–5 people.

Construct a questionnaire suitable for interviewing staff members of the course team.

Interview all staff members of the course team and add articles to the wall display or newsletter. Each group does not need to interview each member of staff.

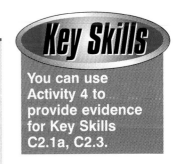

Key Skills

You can use Activity 4 to provide evidence for Key Skills C2.1a, C2.3.

Application of Number

Your Application of Number Key Skills will enable you to do the following.

You must demonstrate your ability in Application of Number by carrying through at least one substantial activity that includes all the straightforward tasks for N2.1, N2.2 and N2.3.

N2.1: Interpret information from *two* different sources, including material containing a graph. You will have provided evidence that you can:

- choose how to obtain the information needed to meet the purpose of your activity

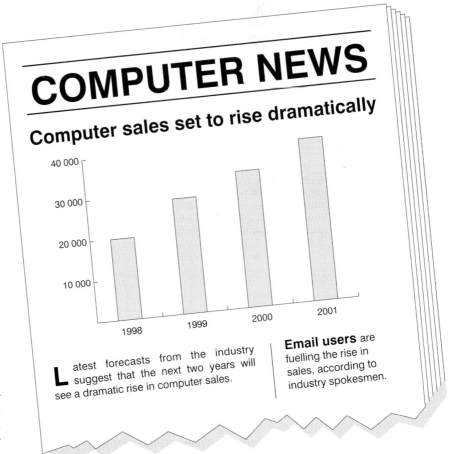

You must demonstrate your ability to interpret information from two different sources – for example, computer magazines

- obtain the relevant information
- select appropriate methods to get the results you need.

N2.2: Carry out calculations to do with amounts and sizes, scales and proportion, handling statistics and using formulae. You will have provided evidence that you can:

- carry out calculations, clearly showing your methods and levels of accuracy
- check your methods to identify and correct any errors, and make sure your results make sense.

N2.3: Interpret the results of your calculations and present your findings. You must use at least *one* graph, *one* chart and *one* diagram. You will have provided evidence that you can:

- select effective ways to present your findings
- present your findings clearly and describe your methods
- explain how the results of your calculations meet the purpose of your activity.

quick fire

What should you do after carrying out a calculation?

Activity 5

This activity may be done individually or in a small group.

A student on this course wishes to buy a computer system to use at home to help with the work for the course.

a Find out the sort of hardware and software needed for the course.
b Find out costs for suitable equipment.
c Submit a costed proposal for three suitable systems:
   • where funds are no problem
   • middle price
   • the cheapest possible system which is still useful.
d Give reasons for your choice.
e Evaluate your work and your working practice.

JARGON DRAGON

By *evaluating* your work you can assess how good your work is. Did you do what was required? How well did you do it? How can you do better next time?

Remember – Application of Number Skills

• Select information and methods to get the results you need.
• Carry out calculations involving two or more steps and numbers of any size, checking the result.
• Present and explain your results.

Information Technology

You will not need to demonstrate Key Skills in IT separately as you will have covered them if you successfully complete units 1 to 3. If you do not complete these units, it is possible for you to claim these skills if you have the necessary proof. To demonstrate your skills in IT you must:

IT2.1: Search for and select information for *two* different purposes. You must provide evidence to show you can:

   • identify the information you need and suitable sources
   • carry out effective searches
   • select information that is relevant to your purpose.

IT2.2: Explore and develop information, and derive new information for *two* different purposes. You must provide evidence to show you can:

- enter and bring together information using formats that help development
- explore information as needed for your purpose
- develop information and derive new information as appropriate.

IT2.3: Present combined information for *two* different purposes. Your work must include at least *one* example of text, *one* example of images and *one* example of numbers. You must provide evidence to show you can:

- select and use appropriate layouts for presenting combined information in a consistent way
- develop the presentation to suit your purpose and the types of information
- ensure your work is accurate, clear and saved appropriately.

Remember – Key Skills

- Communications is a key part of this course.
- Application of Number is a key part of the course.

Activity 6

Make notes about how Key Skills will be taught on your course.

0.4 Course assessment

You will be assessed by having to prove that you can perform certain tasks. To prove this you will have to keep evidence of your skills in a **portfolio**.

JARGON DRAGON

A *portfolio* is a file or folder holding papers, drawings etc.

Activities throughout the units in this textbook work towards your portfolio **evidence** for each unit. Some activities will be practised so that you can get help with your work before producing unaided work for your portfolio, or the work may be used for your portfolio immediately (if it needs to be kept in your portfolio, you will be told). It will then be your responsibility to keep your evidence safe and ready for either internal or external assessment.

You will receive a mark for each of the units you complete and at the end of the course you will be given a grade of Pass, Merit or Distinction. You will be told what evidence you need to produce for each grade. Read the requirements carefully and produce exactly what you are asked for.

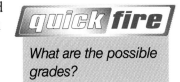

What are the possible grades?

JARGON DRAGON

Producing *evidence* (of a skill or knowledge) means having proof to demonstrate that you have a skill or knowledge.

The evidence may be in the form of:

- documents that you have created
- backup copies of computer files that you have created
- written notes from an assessor to say that they have seen you perform a task correctly.

It is *your* job to keep this portfolio properly. To do this you must:

- keep your portfolio in a safe place
- keep your evidence for each unit of the course and each common skill area separately.

Each piece of evidence should include the following information:

- the unit
- the date it was produced
- the common skill area.

What forms can evidence take?

What information must you put on each item of evidence?

Remember – Portfolio

- Keep your portfolio safe.
- Keep your portfolio up to date.

0.5 Working on your own

You are choosing a vocational course, a course preparing you for work. This is not a course for children who think of themselves and their teachers as 'us and them': it is a course for students prepared to act responsibly and treat their studies as work. You and the staff are members of one course team working towards the same end product – the evidence needed to gain qualifications for the students. Some team members (the staff) have more experience and are more senior to others (the students), and the students must produce the evidence. The staff are there to help you.

Can you look on your studies as work? Can you make the commitment to work and study for 30 hours a week? And this means *working*, not dossing in a classroom or canteen.

Can you organise your own time so that you produce work on time without constant nagging? Can you organise your time so that you work regularly throughout the course, whether you are supervised or not, and not just through the night when the assignment has to be handed in?

Your teachers and lecturers will help you, but the responsibility for the work is yours. Do you think that you will enjoy being responsible for your own work?

The second secret is:

Managing your time

1 Give yourself set working hours. These should include your timetabled hours, but they should add up to 30 hours a week. You know when you want to relax. Make sure that you know when to work. Write yourself a timetable. And *stick to it*.

2 Keep a work diary. You might like to use a desk diary which gives you a page a day, or just use an exercise book – it doesn't matter. List your work tasks for each day. Tick them off as you do them.

3 Start each day by checking your diary. There should be a list of all the jobs to do that day. This will include 'appointments', like going

to the dentist and today's lectures, but also tasks to be completed. In your diary, write an estimate of how long each task will take. When you have completed a task, write down how long it actually took you. You should become more accurate in your estimates as you go along.

4   At the end of the day, review your day. Have you completed all your work? If there are any tasks still to do, write them on another day. List your achievements. What have you learnt today? What have you done today? Did you do it well, adequately or badly. How can you improve for next time?

5   Plan your work. Split major activities into smaller tasks. The tasks might include:

   a *reading* – this includes
      i   reading set by your tutors
      ii reading manuals for interest or for a specific purpose
      iii reading about information technology in books, magazines or newspapers for a specific purpose or for general interest;

   b *listening* to
      i   lectures
      ii explanations from tutors, other students or anyone else
      iii in discussions
      listening means taking in information, not letting words go in one ear and out of the other;

   c other *research* – like
      i   using help screens
      ii getting information on CD-ROM
      iii surfing the Internet;

   d *making notes* can be helpful while reading, listening or doing other research. Many people find it helps them to remember;

   e *planning* your work and thinking about it;

   f *working at the computer* – including
      i   learning and practising with new hardware and software
      ii performing specific tasks on the computer;

   g *writing*.

6   Think about how well you are doing your work.

Remember

You will be assessed on your portfolio for most of your units. Make sure you keep it carefully (and keep backups of all your work).

For your portfolio work you will be told:

- what to do
- how it will be graded
- to evaluate your work.

Always give your work in on time!

Study Skills

Planning Work

To get a merit or a distinction your work has to be completed within the deadline. Here are some suggestions:

1 Do you know what the deadline for the assignment is? If not, ask your teacher.

2 Are you clear what you have to do for the assignment? Get this sorted out first.

3 Write down a list of the stages you need to work through to complete the assignment. This should include doing research at the start and an evaluation at the end, as well as the actual tasks in the assignment. Make sure the stages are in a sensible order – first things first!

4 Write a table like this:

Date	Time	Task	Tick when done
Start			
Deadline			

5 Try to fill in the dates and times with the tasks. Think about your other commitments, such as other assignments you might be doing at the same time. When are college computers available? If you need to interview someone, when is the appointment?

6 Try to plan so that you should finish one or two days before the deadline. Then if something goes wrong and it takes longer than you thought, you will still get it in on time.

7 Remember this is just a *plan*, and things will probably not work out exactly like this. As you do the assignment keep checking the plan and the dates. You will probably need to revise the plan at some point, if tasks go faster or slower than you thought.

Activity 7

a Write down how many hours you think you will spend next week in:
- reading
- listening
- other research
- making notes
- planning your work and thinking about it

- working at the computer
- writing.

Give this estimate to your tutor.

b Next week – keep a diary where you note down, perhaps once an hour, how long you have spent on each of the above activities. Add it up at the end of each day and the end of the week.

c Compare the diary with your original estimate.

Managing your work

You need to find a good place to work. Have you got somewhere to work at home where:

- You will not be disturbed all the time?
- You can spread out your books, papers etc. while you work and don't have to keep shifting them?
- Even better, have you got somewhere where you can leave your work and come back to it later without anything being disturbed?

If there is nowhere suitable at home, then you will have to find somewhere else to do your homework. Maybe somewhere at college or school is open in the evenings and at private study times where you can work without being distracted? Perhaps you could use the local library?

Study Skills

Evaluating your work

For many assignments you need to evaluate your work. Evaluate means find the value of – in other words, you basically have to describe *how good your work is*. Here are some suggestions:

1 How did the planning go? Did you have to alter dates? Why?

2 Did any special problems crop up? What were they? How did you overcome them?

3 What are the best parts of your work? What is so good about them?

4 What are the worst parts of your work? What is wrong with it? How could you have done it better?

/ **Activity 8** /

Discuss in a group how the members of the group like to work.

a Find good places to work on your own in your college or school. Find at least one place for each member of the group where they can work undistracted. If you cannot find a place, discuss it with your tutor.

b Find at least one place for each member of the group to do homework outside your college or school. If you cannot find a place, discuss it with your tutor.

c What materials (books, paper, pens, hardware and software etc.) will you need for work?

d Will you have it in your chosen workplace at college or school? If you don't have the materials you need, what can you do about it?

e Where will you keep your portfolio? How will you keep it safe? How will you remember it when you need it?

Key Terms

After reading through this unit you should understand the following words and phrases. If you do not, go back through the unit and find out, or look them up in the Glossary.

application software
computer communications
evaluation
evidence
grades
hardware

Key Skills
operating system
PC
portfolio
software
vocational course

Test Yourself

1 What units will you study on this course?
2 What Key Skills areas will you cover?
3 What hardware have you used so far?
4 What software have you used?
5 Name two jobs that this course might lead to.
6 What will you cover in Communication Key Skills?
7 What will you cover in Application of Number Key Skills?
8 How will the course be assessed?
9 Name two types of evidence that can be used to demonstrate a skill.
10 What is the secret of success in a task?

Assignment for Unit 0

Work in a group of 3–5 people.

You are going to introduce and explain this course to your parents or other carers.

Decide whether you will do this by inviting them to an event at your school or college or whether you will do it in writing.

You will want to:
* introduce the course team
* introduce the workplace (school or college)
* explain working practices:
  — timetable and own work and study
  — outline of course
  — key skills
  — assessment
* add anything else you think will be of interest.

Plan your event or written material.

Evaluate your work.

Give your work in on time.

Get the Grade!

Here are the criteria against which you will be assessed.

To obtain a pass you must ensure that you:

* collect all the material to introduce the course team (students and staff), introduce the college or school, explain working practices, anything else you think will be of interest
* have a design for the newsletter and plan of how and to whom it will be sent or have a plan for your event.

To obtain a merit you must also ensure that you:

* have come up with a working plan for yourself which you will be able to follow realistically throughout the course
* have worked out a realistic plan for how you will look after your portfolio
* have shown an understanding of key skills and assessment
* have evaluated your work.

To obtain a distinction you must also ensure that you:

* have shown evidence of planning in your work
* have shown evidence of trying to manage your time and of managing your work
* have evaluated your work realistically.

Presenting information

What is covered in this unit

At the end of this unit you will be asked to produce six original documents for different purposes that show a range of writing styles and layouts. You will also have to produce notes describing the documents and comparing two. This unit will guide you through what you need to know to put together this work successfully. You will be assessed on this work and awarded a grade for Unit One.

Materials you will need to complete this unit:

- a variety of formal and informal documents and document templates
- access to computers and printers
- a sophisticated word processor
- a desktop publisher.

Introduction

The most common use of a PC is to create documents. This is because word processing has become the most common way of producing documents in an office. Most people who use a PC for other purposes also print out documents.

JARGON DRAGON

A *PC* – which stands for 'personal computer' – is the most common sort of computer used nowadays. This compares with large expensive mainframe computers used to run large installations like banks and weather forecasts.

In the 1980s it was thought that use of computers would lead to a paperless office as information would be sent electronically. What actually happened is that computers produced much more information than before and this information was often printed. More paper was used than ever before and the 'paperless office' became a joke. In fact a new industry grew up recycling computer paper because there was so much about.

The 'paperless office'!

Activity 1

a Give five reasons why more paper might be used since we started using computers, not less.
b Give one reason why people thought there would be less.

This unit helps you to:

- write original documents in styles that suit your readers
- improve the accuracy and readability of the documents you create
- improve the quality of presentation in documents you create
- choose and apply standard document layouts
- understand and develop good practice in your use of IT.

You will create and compose a variety of **documents** using layouts and styles that suit their different purposes. You will compare the style and layout of documents you originate with similar documents produced by organisations.

JARGON DRAGON

A *document* presents information in a permanent form, usually on paper. The word is also used by many word-processing and desktop-publishing packages to mean an electronic file which may be printed.

When would you need to send a letter rather than a fax?

- A document may be hand written or printed.
- An e-mail or other electronic text file becomes a document when it is printed. For instance, a screen printout or print of a Web page is a document.
- A signed document should have a hand-written signature. (A fax is not a legally signed document as it is a printed copy of a signature.)
- Word-processing packages often call the electronic files they create 'documents'.

The computer programs that can be used to create and organise the information to be presented include:

- Word processors, which are used to create the actual words, or text, in the documents. They include tools to edit the text easily and to check the text for accuracy and readability.
- Graphics and art packages are used to create diagrams and illustrations. The output can be printed or inserted (imported or pasted) into word-processed or desktop-published documents.
- Other packages such as spreadsheets or databases can provide information as text, tables, forms, reports or charts, which can be printed as documents or inserted into a word-processed or desktop-published document.
- Desktop publishers are designed for the presentation of information. They are programs specially designed to create page layouts and will import text and illustrations from other packages as well as allowing text and graphic creation. Printers and publishers who create magazines and newspapers professionally all use desktop publishing.

What does DTP stand for?

What computer packages do

	Desktop publishers	Word processors	Graphics packages	Spreadsheets and databases
Create text	Yes	Main purpose	Yes	Yes
Create information	Yes	Mainly text	Mainly graphic	Main purpose
Create artwork	Yes	Some	Main purpose	Tables, graphs
Create page layout	Main purpose	Yes	Yes	Forms and reports

The table above shows what different computer packages do, but as computer packages get more sophisticated they overlap more and more.

If you are creating a document you usually know what you want to communicate. You also need to think about how you will express your information. There are two things to remember when presenting information.

1 Who is the reader?
2 What is the occasion?

You must learn to:

- use language to suit your reader. For example, when writing for a young child you would use simple words in short sentences, but when writing for an adult you can use longer words and more complicated language
- select a writing style that suits the occasion. For example, the words and sentence length you would use in a letter of complaint would be different from those you'd use in a glossy advertisement.

What is the main purpose of a word-processing package?

1.1 Styles of writing and presentation

The main purpose of a document is to give information to the reader. If you are sending the document, you need to think about the best way of presenting this information.

- You need to think about different writing styles suitable for different readers.
- You may wish to catch the reader's eye.
- You may want to consider how to make the information easy to understand, or how much information to give.
- Sometimes there may even be a legally correct way to give certain information.

Name two important things to remember when presenting information.

Activity 2

For each of the occasions below, choose which style is most appropriate. Why have you chosen that style? What is wrong with the style of the others?

a You apply for a Saturday job in a computer shop

Dear Sir, I am writing to enquire whether you need any extra sales staff on Saturdays. I am currently studying for a GNVQ in Information Technology so I have some knowledge of computers ... etc	**LET ME HELP YOU!** I know ALL about computers! I am a student of Information Technology! **I could sell for you next, and all further, Saturdays!**	To the Manager. Sir, I am a wizz with computers. My Mum and my Dad and my friends ask my advice all the time. I know more than most of your sales people so why don't you give me a Saturday job?

b You send a postcard from holiday to a 5-year-old relative or friend

This is a picture of where we are staying. As you can see, the scenery is pretty spectacular. The journey down was humdrum, which is what is required from such an undertaking. I expect you are keeping yourself busy during your summer vacation. Yours sincerely,	This picture shows the beach here. Lots of sand for building castles. Love,	Flipping smashing place this. Lots of talent on the beach too! I'm learning lots of new chat-up lines. Phoar! See yer,

c The agenda for a meeting of your sports club

Meeting **12 December** **7.30** **Bar of Sports Hall** **BE THERE** **Discuss future events**	To discuss on 12 Dec. 1. Apologies 2. Minutes and matters arising 3. Fixtures for next 3 months 4. New equipment 5. AOB	We have a meeting next Wed at 7.30 to discuss future events and new equipment for the club. As you are on the committee, please try to be there. If you cannot make the meeting, please let me know.

Before creating any document, you will need to consider its purpose.

- Why are you creating this document?
- What do you want the document to communicate?
- Who is the reader ?
- What is the occasion?

You need to change your style of writing to suit your purpose.

- Choose your language to suit your reader. Simple words and short sentences are easier to understand than long words and long sentences. Use short words and sentences if you want your reader to understand something quickly, or if your reader is a young child.

- Use informal language to friends: they may even be amused by the odd joke or swear word and will forgive the odd spelling or grammatical mistake.
- If you do not know your reader you will need to be careful that you do not offend them. You will also need to use more formal language and check your spelling and grammar carefully. Proofread the document.
- If you have complicated information to explain, you will need to use longer sentences and may need to use unusual words. You might need to use technical jargon and to be very accurate in using the correct word to describe something exactly.
- There are standard ways of producing some types of document. Using a standard format will immediately tell the reader what type of information is being conveyed.
- In some cases there may be legally required wording and a wrongly worded document may be invalid.

Give an example of a type of document designed to catch your attention.

Some purposes affect writing style

Attracting attention

> ### ARE YOU TRYING TO ATTRACT ATTENTION?
> Keep it simple.
> Come straight to the point.
> Use clear, concise language.
> Don't give unnecessary detail.
> Make it stand out.

Setting out facts clearly

- Check that the facts are accurate.
- Put each fact down separately.
- Put the facts into a sensible order.
- Explain technical terms.
- Make use of a suitable layout, such as lists, bullet points (like this) or numbering.
- Give examples if they help clarity.

If you were writing an instruction manual for a non-expert reader, what should you do about technical terms and jargon?

Activity 3

a Write a set of instructions for an elderly aunt who has never used a video recorder to record your favourite programme for you.

b What technical terms have you used?

c Does your elderly aunt know what the terms 'Forward/Fast Forward/Rewind/Stop/Pause/Record/Play' mean?

d Discuss your use of technical terms in the instructions.

Ordering/invoicing goods

quick fire

What is the purpose of an invoice?

Business documents must be correctly set out, and should have a heading explaining what they are if the reader is to understand what to do with them (see the figure opposite). The same information, for instance, may be on an order, an invoice and a packing note. The reader must know which type of document it is.

The documents shown in the figure are created this way:

- The customer rings in with an order which is written down on three-part paper.
- The top copy is the order, which is filed.
- The second copy is the packing note, which is sent with the goods ordered. The customer checks the goods against the packing note when they arrive.
- The third copy is the invoice, which is sent to the customer for payment.

quick fire

How would you tell an invoice from a packing note?

```
        ORDER      P105

Customer      Date
JAZ Ltd       12/3/99
High Road
Brickhill

6 bags concrete      6.60
6 bags aggregate     4.80
1 shovel             7.30
                    ─────
                    18.70
         VAT         3.27
                    ─────
       Total        21.37
```

```
    PACKING NOTE       P105

Customer      Date
JAZ Ltd       12/3/99
High Road
Brickhill

6 bags concrete      XXXX
6 bags aggregate     XXXX
1 shovel             XXXX
                    ─────
                     XXXX
         VAT         XXXX
                    ─────
       Total         XXXX
```

```
         INVOICE      P105

Customer      Date
JAZ Ltd       12/3/99
High Road
Brickhill

6 bags concrete      6.60
6 bags aggregate     4.80
1 shovel             7.30
                    ─────
                    18.70
         VAT         3.27
                    ─────
       Total        21.37
```

Three documents holding the same information but performing three different purposes. The documents have their purpose printed at the top. Notice that they all have the same reference number

Organisations may send out hundreds of letters, orders and other documents every day. To help them tell documents apart each will have a reference number. Always quote the reference number when talking or writing to an organisation about a document they sent.

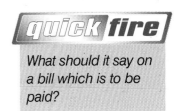

What should it say on a bill which is to be paid?

The needs of your reader

Does your reader have difficulty in reading, perhaps because th[ey are] very old or very young? If so use large clear writing. Is your rea[der in a] hurry? Don't give unnecessary information. For instance, a not[e to a] milkman should say:

3 pints please

It doesn't need an essay about what you usually have, or how m[uch you] like the milk, though politeness (please) is important. It also do[esn't need] to be printed, clear handwriting is fine.

Explaining details

- Your explanations must be clear and easy to follow.
- Your explanation must not be ambiguous. There should be only one possible meaning.
- Write your explanation. Later, perhaps even the next day, read it through. Does it still make sense?
- If the explanation is really complicated, ask a colleague or friend to read it to make sure that it is clear. A good friend will look for errors, and will have done their job well if they find some, so don't get annoyed if they do.

Summarising information

Don't repeat it all. Don't give new examples. Repeat the main points. Use language to suit the reader and choose the right words for the job. Select a writing style that suits the occasion, and use sentence length and complexity to convey your meaning.

Activity 4

Think about the following examples of different types of document.

- A letter responding to a job advertisement.
- An agenda for a meeting for a sports or social club.
- Minutes of a meeting for a sports or social club.
- An advertisement trying to sell something second-hand.
- A note to the milkman ordering milk.
- A formal invitation to a social event.
- A glossy advertisement for some new cosmetics.
- A letter to a newspaper.
- A table of results for a sporting activity.
- A fax header sheet.

What style of writing will you use for each? Choose:

	A	or	B
1	hand-written		printed
2	formal		informal
3	long words and sentences		short words and sentences
4	need to attract attention		use a standard layout

Tools

There are computer **tools** to help you with your style of writing, including **spell checkers**, **grammar checkers**, **readability checkers**, a **thesaurus**, and **templates** for different types of documents.

JARGON DRAGON

Part of a computer program such as a word processor which gives extra help to the user, but which is not essential to the purpose of the program, is a *computer tool*.

A *template* is a document containing layout information.

Templates

You can set up your own template, for instance one containing your address and telephone number for writing your letters. Some word processors and desktop publishers have standard templates, or have **wizards** which help you set up a template by offering different options.

Organisations sometimes have standard templates which all employees are expected to use.

JARGON DRAGON

A *wizard* is a computer tool that helps you do fairly complicated things by asking questions.

Spell checkers

Many programs now come with spell checkers. They are extremely useful but should be used with care. Make sure that you are using a dictionary for the correct language. You will probably want a dictionary for British English or International English rather than US English.

The spell checker will only see whether the word is in the dictionary and not whether the spelling is correct for the context. For example, if you have spelt 'for' as 'fur' it will not be picked up as incorrect. It will not tell whether to use 'no' or 'know'. You might need to use a printed dictionary as well.

Spell checkers will also pick up proper names and give some amusing suggestions. If you use the names often it is worth adding them to your dictionary. Most spell checkers allow you to add words to the dictionary, to save it correcting proper names the whole time.

JARGON DRAGON

You check the spelling of words in your document against a standard dictionary using a *spell checker*.

A *grammar checker* checks the grammar of a document against set rules. However, it doesn't check for meaning.

Grammar checkers

Many word processors also come with grammar checkers. They will pick up repeated words words, and check that full stops are followed by a capital letter. also they check that you don't make mistakes such as 'I is . . .' and that your sentences don't get too long and convoluted.

Grammar checkers sometimes are used with readability checkers, which decide how easy the document is to understand. This is done using a formula based on word length and sentence length.

Give an example of a correct spelling that a spell checker would pick up as an error.

The readability index can often be set for the type of document that you are writing, so the grammar checking tool picks up different 'errors' in a business letter than it would in advertising, for instance.

JARGON DRAGON

In a *readability check* the computer checks for the 'reading age' of a piece of writing (i.e. how easy it is to understand).

A *thesaurus* offers other words with similar meaning.

All these tools are very useful but are no substitute for good proofreading of a document. Only a person can check whether your document makes sense. Only *you* can check that it says what you meant to say.

Activity 5

a List six purposes of presenting information that will affect the style of presentation.

b Give an example of using a thesaurus.

Activity 6

Check out the tools available on your word-processing program. Make sure that you know how all of them work.

a Write a handout for a Year 7 pupil, explaining how to use one tool. If you do this activity as a group, then each one in the group should choose a different tool.

b Choose and use a writing style suitable for a pupil in their first year at secondary school. You may use material from the Help screens or from manuals as well as your own words.

c Keep dated drafts of your work to show how you progress and hand these in with your final work.

d Make notes on your drafts of how you will improve it. Hand in a note with your final work saying what you think you have done well, and what you are less happy with. Always check your work. Give your work in on time.

Always check your work

Standard checks to make on your work are given below.

1 Spell check to correct spelling and some other mistakes. A spell checker *will* detect
   a words spelt incorrectly
   b repeated words such as 'and and'.

It will *not*:

c find the correct spelling out of several possible spellings – there or their; to, two or too

d understand abbreviations such as GNVQ

e understand proper names – e.g. Darren – though you might be able to add your own abbreviations and proper names to the dictionary.

2 Grammar check to:

a make sure that sentences have a subject and verb that agree

b find out the level of reading difficulty of your work

c detect sentences ending with two full stops

d detect sentences not starting with a capital letter

e check your writing style to make sure it is easy to understand – for instance

i that you use the active rather than passive tense. This means that the sentence says the subject did something, rather than something was done to the subject. A sentence in the active voice says 'The dog bit the man.' A sentence in the passive voice says 'The man was bitten by the dog'

ii that you use a style suitable for your purpose. It will offer several styles for you to choose from.

3 Proofread by eye on screen to:

a find mistakes missed by the spell checker

b check that your writing makes sense

c check that your document meets your purpose.

4 Use print preview to check the page layouts of your document to make sure that it looks good before printing. Check your punctuation marks.

5 Proofread the printed page as a further check.

6 For important documents, get a friend or colleague to check the printed page before you issue it.

Give an example of a spelling mistake that a spell checker will not pick up.

Name three different types of checks to make on a document before sending it out.

Activity 7

List the tools on your word processor. What tool would you use to check the reading age of a document?

1.2 Types of information

The type of information you are trying to convey will also affect how it is presented. You might find it best just to use straightforward words, or it may be helpful to use a picture or diagram. When giving numerical information it is worth thinking if this is easier to understand in a table, or illustrated by a graph.

How many different types of information can you see on the noticeboard in the figure on page 32?

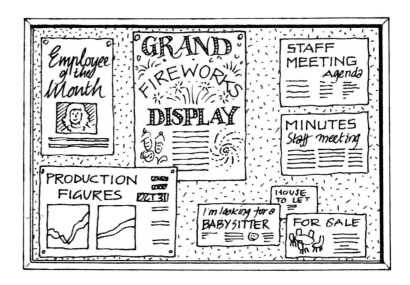

Information in different forms

Name five types of information.

Information in the form of text

This is the most common form of information. It is just words.

Information in the form of charts and graphs

These can be used to illustrate points made in the text, or can give information on their own. If they are used on their own, they should have clear headings and explanatory labelling.

Information in the form of numbers

What type of information might be useful, apart from text, to explain to someone how to get from the railway station to your house?

If there are several numbers, it is probably best to give them in some sort of table. It is often very helpful to use a chart or graph to illustrate numerical information.

Information in the form of graphics

You may have heard the saying, 'A picture is worth a thousand words.' Certainly a good illustration can show something that needs many words to describe. However, a graphic should be relevant in a document and not just used because you have that particular piece of clip art.

Activity 8

Check out the graphic facilities available on your computer system.

a Find what clip art is available, and how to use it. What packages are available for you to produce your own artwork?

b Find out if there is a scanner available for your use. If there is, find out how to use it.

c Write instructions for using the scanner for a senior manager who is not used to using computers.

d Print out an invitation to your next birthday party using appropriate artwork. Include graphics within the work. Choose a style of writing and presentation suitable to the type of person you will invite. Write notes explaining your choice of style.

e Write a note explaining how you generated the graphics in your invitation.

Information in the form of tables

Tables allow you to format your document into rows and columns. They are particularly useful for presenting numerical information. Most word processors have some sort of facility for forming tables.

What type of information would you use if you wanted to take public transport to a holiday destination?

Activity 9

Check out tables in your word-processing package.

An ice cream company wanted to make comparisons on its sales of ice cream over 4 years. Its sales (in millions of ice creams) were:

1995:	24	Jan-Feb	1996:	33	Jan-Feb
	47	Mar-Apr		50	Mar-Apr
	96	May-Jun		83	May-Jun
	124	Jul-Aug		156	Jul-Aug
	108	Sep-Oct		98	Sep-Oct
	35	Nov-Dec		23	Nov-Dec
1997:	47	Jan-Feb	1998:	56	Jan-Feb
	79	Mar-Apr		102	Mar-Apr
	145	May-Jun		135	May-Jun
	203	Jul-Aug		208	Jul-Aug
	126	Sep-Oct		76	Sep-Oct
	45	Nov-Dec		51	Nov-Dec

a Put this information into a table to make it easier to read.

b Experiment with shading the table, perhaps alternate rows or alternate columns. Is this any easier to read?

c Experiment with justifying columns left, right and centred to see if this makes it clearer.

d Try various layouts to see which you think is clearest.

e Discuss your results round the class.

1.3 Document layout

Make a collection of various documents that you can obtain. Good sources can be

- your workplace if you have a job
- your parents or carers and their workplaces
- other relatives and friends and their workplaces
- any sent directly to you, for instance a letter from your college offering you a place.

These can include letters, order forms, invoices, delivery notes, notices about meetings, minutes of meetings, newsletters, memos, instructions, newspapers, magazines or anything else you have.

Use them later in this unit when considering different document layouts.

Some types of documents

Memos

A **memo** (short for memorandum) is an informal document used within an organisation. A memo should say right at the top that it is a memo, an internal note to be acted upon. It should say who it is to, who it is from, who else is getting a copy (cc.) and what its subject is. This immediately tells the reader how important the memo is. It must also be dated.

Memos should be fairly short and to the point, so they need not be on a full sheet of A4 – A5 is often big enough. Small memo sheets are often in landscape rather than portrait format so that the same heading can be used for both sheet sizes.

MEMORANDUM
To: Date:
From:
Cc:
SUBJECT _____

A typical memo layout

Agenda

An **agenda** tells a person attending a meeting what will be discussed at that meeting. It should be headed 'agenda' and the matters to be discussed should be listed. It is also helpful to say which meeting the agenda is for. A copy should be made available to all members.

> **COMPANY TABLE TENNIS CLUB COMMITTEE**
> Meeting: Thursday 22nd November 5.30 in Social Club
> AGENDA
>
> 1. Apologies
> 2. Minutes of the last meeting
> 3. Matters Arising
> 4. Correspondence
> 5. Secretary's Report
> 6. Treasurer's Report
> 7. Christmas Social
> 8. Winter league
> 9. Next year's fixtures
> 10. Any Other Business

A typical agenda

Newsletter

Newsletters are informal printed reports giving information that is of interest to a specific group of people – members of a club, customers of a business, employees of an organisation, fans of a sports team or pop group, for example. It needs to be attractive and easy to read and aimed at the interests of the reader group.

Which computer package is designed primarily for creating page layouts?

Some typical newsletters

Electronic mail

Electronic messages (**e-mails**) can be sent through local networks or over the Internet.

An e-mail screen

Publicity flyers

A flyer is a single-sheet advertisement, usually about A5 size, which is designed to attract members of the public to an event or to buy a product.

Giving out flyers

Business cards

Small personal cards about 8.5 cm × 5.5 cm are often handed out to other people. The **business card** holds information about:

- the person they belong to (their name and position)
- the organisation the person is representing (name, address and what they do)
- anything else required.

Large organisations give cards to their employees who have contact with their customers. Giving a business card is a quick way of giving information and the company image.

Cards can be very useful for small businesses as well as large ones

Minutes

Minutes are an official record of what is decided at a meeting. The minutes of the previous meeting are usually discussed at the start of the next one. People attending the meeting agree that they are correct, or amend them if they are not. The person chairing (i.e. running) the meeting signs them as correct. People can ask questions about items in the minutes under the agenda item 'matters arising'.

Itineraries

If an employee of an organisation goes on a business trip, the organisation often makes the travel plans and buys the tickets. Before the journey the employee is given the tickets and a list of the travel arrangements. This list is called an **itinerary**. It should contain:

- dates, times and places of departure and arrival of planes and trains
- names and addresses and telephone numbers of hotels booked together with dates of bookings
- any other information needed.

Screen display

A **screen display** is what appears on a computer screen. The design of a computer screen for data entry or for data output should be given as much thought as any permanent document.

An employee going on a business trip is given a list of trains to catch. What is this document called?

COMPANY TABLE TENNIS CLUB COMMITTEE

Minutes of meeting held on Thursday 22nd November 5.30 in The Social Club

Present: Zaheer Abass, Stevie Flowers, Jane Fowler, John Griggs, Pat Jenkins.

Apologies: Ella Yo.

1. The minutes of the last meeting were agreed as a true record.
2. Matters arising: None
3. A list of correspondence had been circulated. It was all straight forward and the meeting was happy with the way that the secretary had handled it.
4. The secretary's report had been circulated and accepted.
5. The treasurer's report had been circulated. His figures were accepted but he was asked to look for a bank account which offered better interest.
6. JF reported on the arrangements for the Christmas Social which are now all in place. There are still a few tickets left. She will send a reminder to members who have not yet bought any.
7. The winter league matches have already started. Results are posted on the notice board. So far there are no problems.
8. ZA has written to all the usual match opponents. Dates and venues have been agreed with all except two whom he will chase.

   PJ suggested we try to set up a fixture against the police team. ZA to follow up.
9. PJ suggested a recruitment drive in the new year. Agreed. PJ and JF to bring plans to the next meeting.
10. Meeting closed 7.00pm

Typical minutes

Itinerary
Ms Claire Mitchell's visit to London
10 September 2000

0745	Depart Newport Station
0915	Arrive Paddington Station London
1030	Meeting with Mr James Watson of:
	J S Millbank
	16 Fairview Road
	Wembley
	London
	Tel: 0181 xxx xxxx
1230	Meeting and lunch with Ms Lorraine Carr of:
	Nelson Books Ltd
	20 Montpleasant View Road
	Kensal Rise
	London
	Tel: 0171 xxx xxxx
1720	Depart Paddington Station
1840	Arrive Newport Station

A typical itinerary

A screen display is what appears on a computer screen

Business letters

A **business letter** is a formal document and should be printed on letter-headed paper. The letter heading will contain the name and address of the business plus any other information that the company wishes to give.

Datafit Fax

Unit 15, Leeway Industrial Park,
Canal Road, Huntingdon HSP 7PT

Fax: +44 1480 xxx xxxx
Tel: +44 1480 xxx xxxx
email: xxx.xxx@compuserve.com

Claire Mitchell
Books for Life Publishers
16 Station Road
Newport
NP16 4SY

20 September 2000

Dear Ms Mitchell

Your ref: DF/867463

We will be delighted to meet you at our offices at 11.30 a.m. on 15 September to discuss your office's requirements for fax machines. Please call at our Reception desk and ask for me. I have arranged for our sales director, James Henderson, to attend our meeting.

I look forward to seeing you.

Yours sincerely

Jennifer Parsons
Sales Account Executive

Typical business letter

Business letters contain reference numbers (senders and recipient), the date it is written, the name and address of the recipient as well as the actual letter.

Any organisation is likely to have a standard format for their letters.

Fax header pages

A **fax** ('facsimile') is a copy of a document sent over a telephone line. This is done by feeding an existing document into a fax machine, or by sending a document stored on a computer file over a telephone line using a modem.

The fax machine, or computer simulating a fax machine, must be switched on at the receiving end for the copy to be successfully transmitted. This is unlike e-mail, where the message is stored until it is read.

Organisations sending a fax are likely to have a header page to send with each fax giving information about the organisation.

Give one advantage and one disadvantage of using e-mail instead of a fax.

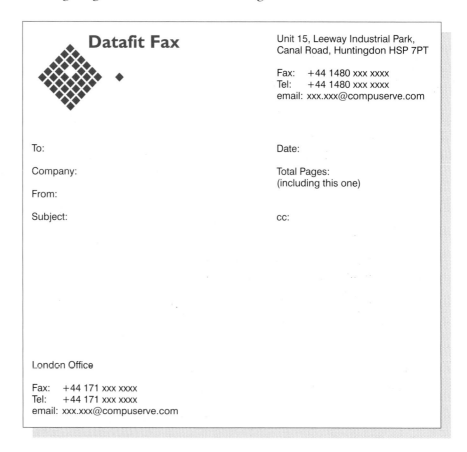

Datafit Fax

Unit 15, Leeway Industrial Park,
Canal Road, Huntingdon HSP 7PT

Fax: +44 1480 xxx xxxx
Tel: +44 1480 xxx xxxx
email: xxx.xxx@compuserve.com

To:

Company:

From:

Subject:

Date:

Total Pages:
(including this one)

cc:

London Office

Fax: +44 171 xxx xxxx
Tel: +44 171 xxx xxxx
email: xxx.xxx@compuserve.com

Typical fax header sheet

Reports

A report is a formal document written for a purpose, such as describing an investigation. A report will need:

- title page, containing
  - title of report
  - name/s of author/s

- date of writing
  - person or people asking for report
- contents page
- terms of reference (the purpose of the report)
- investigation procedure (how you found the information in the report)
- findings (the main part of the report, i.e. the information you discovered)
- conclusions (short summary of the information giving the main findings)
- acknowledgements:
  - list of people helping with the report
  - list of books and magazines, etc. used
- appendices of raw data used in report – for example:
  - the questionnaire if you did a survey
  - publicity material given to you.

Activity 11

Here is a list of documents and their descriptions.

1 agenda	**A** a formal note from one person to another
2 business card	**B** lists the items to be discussed in a meeting
3 business letter	**C** a few pages giving news of what is happening in the organisation sending the document
4 e-mail	**D** sheet of paper advertising something
5 fax header page	**E** small piece of cardboard giving name and position of someone working in an organisation and how they can be contacted
6 itinerary	**F** a message sent electronically by one computer user to another
7 memo	**G** a record of what has been discussed at a meeting
8 minutes	**H** what shows up on a visual display unit
9 newsletter	**I** programme of travel arrangements for a journey
10 publicity flyer	**J** a formal summary of information discovered from an investigation or by research
11 report	**K** front page giving information about sender added to documents copied over the telephone system
12 screen display	**L** formal letter from or to an organisation

Match each document with the correct description.

Layouts

Most types of documents used within a company will have standard layouts. These layouts are often similar between different organisations. The different features of layout are listed below.

Page size and orientation

Standard size for paper in Europe is A4, which is 297 mm × 210 mm. If you fold this in half you get A5, which is 210 mm × 148 mm. If you double the page size you get A3, which is 420 mm × 297 mm.

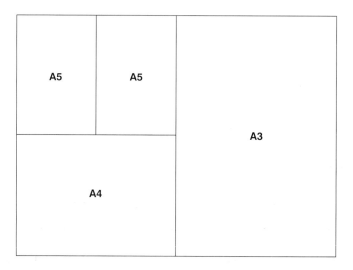

Paper sizes. Note that two times A5 gives A4 and two times A4 gives A3. Two times A3 gives A2, but few college printers will print this size of paper

How big is A5 relative to A3?

Your word-processing package may offer other standard **page sizes** (such as letter, legal, B4, envelope) and you can check these out by trying to change the page set-up. The types of page size allowed by your word processor will depend on the paper your printer can cope with.

Newsletters are often printed on large sheets and folded up. Letters and reports are usually printed on A4 or a similar size. Shorter amounts of information may be printed on smaller sheets of paper to save money, for instance many organisations use A5 sheets for memos.

Would you make a business card landscape or portrait?

Page orientation means which way up the page is. There are two possibilities:

- *portrait* is longer than it is wide – for instance, A4 portrait is 297 mm long and 210 mm wide
- *landscape* is wider than it is long – A4 landscape is 210 mm long and 297 mm wide.

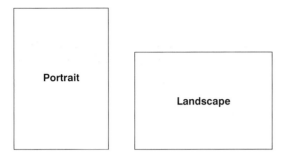

Page orientation

Line spacing

In word processors, most text is single spaced, i.e. one line follows

another, like the lines in most of this book. It is also possible to have

double spacing like the lines in this paragraph. Here there is a blank line

between each printed line. This is often used for drafts to allow plenty of

space for corrections.

Line spacing can also be 1½, as in this paragraph, where there is blank

space the depth of half a line between each printed line. Other spacings

are also possible. Experiment with your word-processing package to see

how different spacing look.

Paragraph format

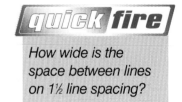

How wide is the space between lines on 1½ line spacing?

Apart from spacing in terms of line height, most word processors and all desktop publishers allow you to set the space before and after paragraphs. This is usually set in points, where there are 72 points per inch or just above 28 points per centimetre. Like many terms in word processing and desktop publishing, the word 'points' goes back to the time when printing was done by setting out letters made of lead in a wooden frame. This section has had the white spaces between paragraphs increased. They are further apart than in the rest of the book.

The previous paragraph had an indent for the first line of the paragraph; that is, the paragraph started in from the left-hand side. This paragraph has a hanging indent – the rest of the paragraph after the first line has been pushed in.

Usually all the lines of text line up at the left-hand edge. This is called left **justification** and leaves a ragged edge on the right. If it is lined up on the right-hand edge it is called right justification and the left-hand edge is ragged. When both right and left justification are used the text is said to be fully justified. Text can also be centred.

This text is left justified. It has a straight edge on the left and a ragged edge on the right. It is the usual way to write letters and reports.	This text is right justified. It lines up on the right and is ragged on the left. It is rarely used for text as it looks odd, but is useful for lining up numbers like this: 27 1035 18
This text is fully justified lining up on both the right and left hand side. It is a common format for books and newsletters as it looks very neat. In order to get different length words fitting exactly at both ends. white spaces of different sizes are added between words and letters in words.	This is centred text and can be very effective on posters.

Text justifications

If you are writing a long document using more than one page, you need to make sure that paragraphs which are split between pages do not have only one or two lines on one page, and the rest of the paragraph on another. The small part of the paragraphs split in this way are called 'widows', where the first line is on the bottom of one page and the rest of the paragraph on the top of the next page. 'Orphans' occur when most of the paragraph is at the bottom of one page and just the last line is at the top of the next.

What is a widow?

Activity 12

Check out the desktop publisher in your college. How does it compare with the word processor for

a Ease of editing text and artwork? List the differences, if any.
b Ease of importing text and artwork? List the differences, if any.
c Changing paragraph formats? List the different formats for each package.

Headers and footers

Headers can be placed at the top of every page. They contain information such as the title of the document or the title of the section of the document so the reader can locate places in the text quickly. In a long document the headers on the right-hand page may be different from the headers on the left-hand page.

Footers are placed at the bottom of the page, and can contain the page number, the date the page was written, the name of the page's author, the filename of the document on disk – or any other useful information. Again, the information in the footer is often an office standard.

What information is presented in the headers and footers of this book?

Headers and footers might not show on the screen, or may show faintly on the screen while you are word processing a document.

Margins

Text does not usually go right to the edge of the page – blank space is left at the top, bottom, left and right. These blank edges are called the **margins**. Some page designs have very wide margins to improve the appearance of the work.

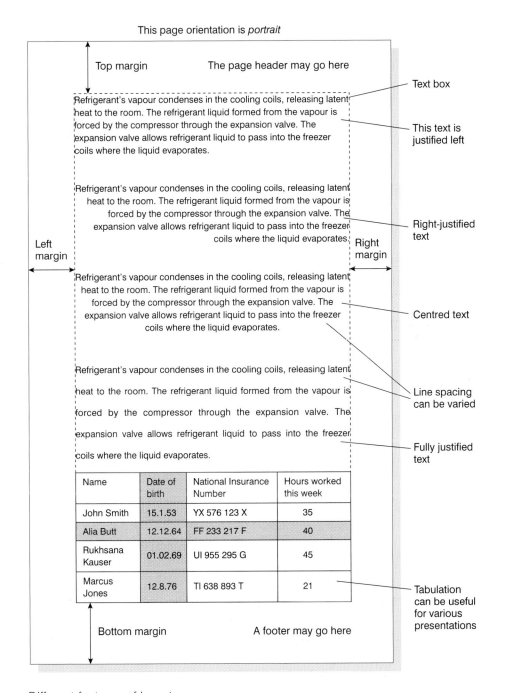

This page orientation is portrait

Top margin — The page header may go here

— Text box

Refrigerant's vapour condenses in the cooling coils, releasing latent heat to the room. The refrigerant liquid formed from the vapour is forced by the compressor through the expansion valve. The expansion valve allows refrigerant liquid to pass into the freezer coils where the liquid evaporates. — This text is justified left

Refrigerant's vapour condenses in the cooling coils, releasing latent heat to the room. The refrigerant liquid formed from the vapour is forced by the compressor through the expansion valve. The expansion valve allows refrigerant liquid to pass into the freezer coils where the liquid evaporates. — Right-justified text

Left margin | Right margin

Refrigerant's vapour condenses in the cooling coils, releasing latent heat to the room. The refrigerant liquid formed from the vapour is forced by the compressor through the expansion valve. The expansion valve allows refrigerant liquid to pass into the freezer coils where the liquid evaporates. — Centred text

Refrigerant's vapour condenses in the cooling coils, releasing latent heat to the room. The refrigerant liquid formed from the vapour is forced by the compressor through the expansion valve. The expansion valve allows refrigerant liquid to pass into the freezer coils where the liquid evaporates. — Line spacing can be varied

— Fully justified text

Name	Date of birth	National Insurance Number	Hours worked this week
John Smith	15.1.53	YX 576 123 X	35
Alia Butt	12.12.64	FF 233 217 F	40
Rukhsana Kauser	01.02.69	UI 955 295 G	45
Marcus Jones	12.8.76	TI 638 893 T	21

— Tabulation can be useful for various presentations

Bottom margin — A footer may go here

Different features of layout

Fonts

The **font** is the type of lettering used.

This paragraph is printed in Times font. It is a *serif* font. Serif fonts are considered easier to read than fonts without the serifs. They are often used in newspapers, books and newsletters.

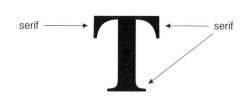

This is a letter T printed in a sans-serif font

This is a letter T printed in a serif font

serif ⟶   serif

The serifs are the sticking out bits at the ends of lines in the letters

Give an example of a sans serif font

This paragraph is printed in Helvetica, a sans serif font. Sans-serif fonts are considered more 'modern' looking than fonts with serifs and many businesses use them for their letters.

There are large numbers of other fonts available.

Font size

The size of the font can be changed:

This is 12 point

this is 8 point

Which font is larger – 10 point or 20 point?

this is 36 point.

Activity 13

Check out the fonts and sizes available on your word processor and desktop publisher, also any font enhancements relating to font styles such as **bold**, <u>underline</u>, superscript etc. Choose suitable fonts and create:

a A list of ten useful formulae to learn for maths and science GCSEs such as Πr^2 and H_2O.
b A flyer for a new hair studio.
c An order form for a mail order company selling T-shirts featuring a slogan of your choice.
d A notice for what to do in case of fire.

Standard layouts

Organisations like to project a consistent image. They will have a similar style of presentation for all documents sent out – headed notepaper, compliments slips, business cards and newsletters. They often insist on standard layouts for the same reason.

Another reason for standard layouts, for internal as well as external documents, is that they are easy to read. Always putting a letter reference number on the top left of a page makes it easy to find, for instance.

Activity 14

a Look at the documents that you collected in Activity 10. Have a look at the position on the page of
- the company logo
- the date of the document
- any headings
- the name of the addressee
- any reference numbers
- the signature of the sender.

b Which of the above items would you put on the following types of document, and where would you put them?
1. a business letter
2. a business newsletter
3. an internal memo
4. an agenda for an internal meeting
5. minutes of a meeting
6. an order form
7. an invoice
8. a delivery note
9. an advertisement for the organisation.
Give reasons for your choice.

c Why do you think commercial organisations use standard layouts for their documents?

1.4 Presentation techniques

It is important to present information clearly. Poorly presented information may annoy or confuse readers. They may misunderstand the information, or even stop reading it.

In a long document be consistent with

- font styles
- headings and subheadings

- bullets and numbering
- italics, boldness and underlining
- page formatting
- indentation
- line spacing
- footnotes.

This will help the reader's comprehension, and they will be able to find what they are looking for more easily.

Before creating a document *always* think about what you want to achieve with it.

- What is its purpose?
- Who is it meant for?
- What format will appeal to the readers?
- How will you design the document?

The features of word-processing and desktop-publishing packages are those which have always been used by publishers and printers, even before the days of computers. They are there to help you design the look of the documents you produce.

You should really have a clear idea of the look of each page before producing it, and you might find it helpful to rough out a page layout by hand before starting work at the computer. This is especially useful if you are short of time at the keyboard.

Ideally you produce the text, using a word processor, and the illustrations using art packages, before the final desktop publishing. This allows you to think separately about

- what to say and
- how to say it.

This section is really about 'how to say it', although we do need to know 'what to say' first.

What to say

Before you start . . .

You know the purpose of the document – but:

- Do you need to attract the reader, or is the reader waiting for the information?
- How long should the document be?
- How much information is involved?
- Do you have all the information you need, or must you do some research first? If so, what do you need to research and how and when will you do it?

- Is there a legal format to the document?
- Has your organisation got a standard format for the document?
- Is the information easy to understand as text alone or does it need illustrations (pictures, diagrams, tables, graphs)?
- Will illustrations help, even if they are not strictly necessary?
- How easily does the reader learn by reading?
- How formal should the text be?
- Is humour appropriate and helpful?

What do you want to say?

Gather together all the information that you need for your document. This will include:

- the results of any research that you have done
- text that you have already written
- text that you obtain from someone else
- original text that you must create
- illustrations that you have already
- illustrations that you need from someone else
- illustrations that you must create.

How will you combine all these forms of information? What order should it come in? You will need a consistent style. This may involve altering information received from elsewhere. You may need to copy or scan information into electronic format, or edit information received in electronic format.

How to say it

There are many features that you can use to help create effective documents. You will need to know how and when to use all the techniques described in this section in a document. You will probably need to create a number of documents before you use them well.

Layout grid

A **layout grid** divides your page up into a grid of squares of known size and helps you to decide the layout of your page.

You will have one in a desktop-publishing program, you might have one in a word processor or you can create one by using squared paper.

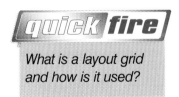

What is a layout grid and how is it used?

Titles and headings

Where do you want **titles** and **headings**, and what size do you want them? Will you want subheadings? You will need to decide sizes and styles of titles and headings, the size probably being in proportion to the importance of the heading. For a clean, unfussy look it is a good idea not to use too many different fonts.

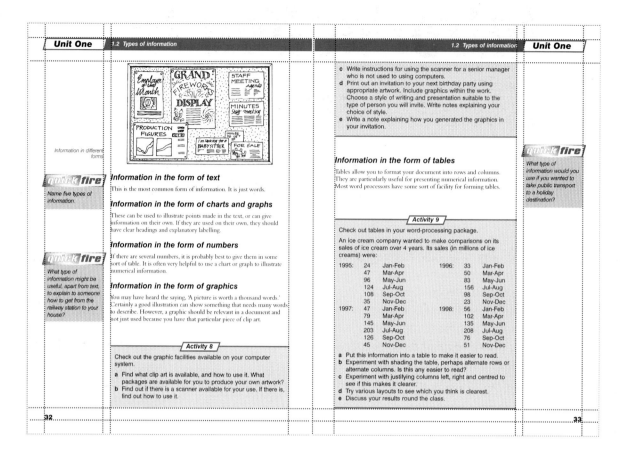

Using a layout grid while designing this book

Hanging indents

Paragraphs can be indented from the right, from the left or both. In paragraphs that are right indented the whole paragraph is always moved towards the left on a page.

JARGON DRAGON

Indentation – when text does not go right to the edge of the page.

Paragraphs that are left indented may have the whole paragraph indented, or may have only the first line indented (first line indent) or may have the whole paragraph except the first line indented (**hanging indent**).

Introduction to GNVQ Information Technology ← Chapter title

0.1 What is a GNVQ? ← A head

Information technology students ← Caption

Where does the course lead? ← B head

Jobs in IT can be divided into three types ← C head

Titles and headings used in this book

Right indent	Full left indent	First line left indent	Left hanging indent
This paragraph has not been indented.	This paragraph has not been indented.	This paragraph has not been indented.	This paragraph has not been indented.
This paragraph has been right indented. It has been indented by half a centimetre.	This paragraph has been left indented. It has been indented by half a centimetre.	This paragraph has been left indented (first line only). It has been indented by half a centimetre.	This paragraph has been left indented using a hanging indent. It has been indented by half a centimetre.

Indentation

Subscript and superscript

Subscripts and **superscripts** are often used in formulae in technical documents. This is a $_{subscript}$. This is a ^{superscript}.

Borders and shading

> Bits of text may have borders round them.

> Bits of text may be shaded.

Borders and shading can be used to emphasise the text and make it more interesting. You might like to think about their use in this book.

Justification

Text may be left, right or fully justified, or centred. It is very much a matter of taste and fashion.

Headers and footers

These are very useful on a document as they give information outside the main body of the text. For instance, on any page in this book you can always see what unit you are in.

What is a footer?

It is standard in most offices to use a footer with the name under which the word-processed document has been stored on computer and the date it was created or last edited.

Templates

A template is a pattern or guide to help you make something. A document template holds information about the layout of the document and items such as a company logo or form outline, which is always on the document.

An organisation that uses standard formats for their documents should issue their computer users with templates. It is possible to make your own templates on a word processor and desktop publisher.

Fonts and sizes

Different fonts and sizes are used within a document to emphasise parts of it, depending on how readable it must be and how much it needs to attract attention.

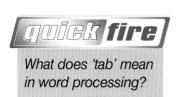

What does 'tab' mean in word processing?

Tables and tabs

These are used to arrange fairly complex information on a page.

Graphics

There is a saying that a picture is worth a thousand words. A graphic – whether a picture, diagram, map, graph or chart – can often make clear something that is very hard to put into words. It can also be used to help make a text more inviting.

However, if not used sensibly graphics can also act as a distraction. So think carefully about the use of graphic items.

Using a graphic to emphasise text

Dividing lines (rules)

Vertical lines are used between columns on a page and horizontal lines are used across the page to divide it up.

Columns

Text can also be set into two or more columns on a page, as in a newspaper. This section has been set in three columns with dividing lines.

This makes it easier to have a lot of separate items on one page, and it makes a lot of text on large paper easier to read and find one's way around.

It is often used for large pages such as newspapers, magazines and newsletters.

The columns do not have to be the same size as each other. For instance, in this book we use a narrow column and a wide column.

Charts and graphs

These are very useful for showing numerical data graphically. Provided they are properly used they illustrate and emphasise the different sizes of numbers much better than any text.

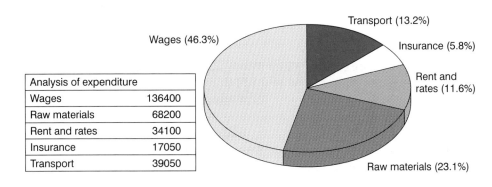

Analysis of expenditure	
Wages	136400
Raw materials	68200
Rent and rates	34100
Insurance	17050
Transport	39050

The pie chart shows the relative differences in expenditure much better than the table, but the table shows it more accurately

53

Use of white space

Blank space between the text and pictures is used to emphasise the text and make the page more attractive.

Bold and italic text

Bold and *italic* text can be used together with <u>underlined</u> text, CAPITALS and different fonts and sizes to pick out particular words and sections of text.

Upper and lower case

UPPER CASE is often used for emphasis – lower case is supposed to be easier to read.

Colour

Adding colour to documents can make them very much more attractive. It can be used for emphasising text and can transform artwork. It is, however, much more expensive to print.

Bulleted lists

Bullets have many uses:

- They can be used to make several points.
- They make each point separately.
- They emphasise each point better than writing them next to each other in the text.
- You can choose what to use as your bullet point to make the list look attractive.

What is meant by a bullet in printing?

Special symbols

You often need symbols that might not be on your keyboard and you need to know how to insert them into your text. Here are a few:

£ Π ∞ ♣ ♥   ™ √ ⇨ ↗ ↘ □ ○ ▲ ▼ ◆ ✓ ✗ ☆

You may also use special symbols or logos to point to particular parts of a text.

Symbols and logos used in this textbook

Contents and indexes

For a long document, you will need a **table of contents** at the start, where you list what is in the document and where it is.

An **index** at the back, where readers can look up points they are interested in, is also useful.

How would you look up in this book what a spreadsheet is for?

The list at the front of a book showing the subject matter of the book is called the *table of contents*.

The alphabetical list at the end of a book, indicating where in the book subjects can be found, is the *index*.

Case study

Sophie's sandwiches

Johnny and Sophie work at a boatbuilder's employing about 80 people. It is on the river about 20 minutes walk from the nearest shops and there is no canteen. Most people bring a packed lunch. Johnny always brought jam sandwiches and looked enviously at Sophie's delicious looking lunches. He persuaded her to bring two lunches and he paid her for her trouble. Other people in the company thought this a good idea and Sophie's sandwiches became very popular. However, there was a limit to the number of sandwiches she wanted to bring in every day so Johnny suggested that he and Sophie ask the managing director of the company if she could set up a sandwich bar for the workforce, being given space and time by the company to run it.

ⓠ *Help Sophie and Johnny to decide how to write a letter to the managing director, Jake Oliver, who is similar in character to the head of your educational establishment.*

ⓠ *Answer the questions in the section 'Before you start . . .' on page 48.*

ⓠ *List the information that Sophie and Johnny need, and help them gather it together.*

ⓠ *Go through the three processes (before you start, what you want to say, how to say it) on pages 48–49 with the boss's reply to Sophie and Johnny.*

a Find a job advertisement in your local paper that you would like to apply for. Write the letter of application.

b With a partner, choose a newspaper or magazine which you both enjoy. Write a report analysing its style and presentation.

Choose and use a writing style suitable for your task

1.5 Standard ways of working

Many organisations have rules and guidelines to help people work effectively and avoid problems. These are known as 'standard ways of working'.

Standards are used to make sure that work can be done

- well
- quickly
- safely

and that it isn't

- lost
- stolen
- damaged.

It is especially easy in IT to lose work, or for other people to misuse your work.

Standards should make sure that you can do the following:

1 Manage your work effectively. Because it is so easy to correct your work in IT, many people working with computers do not plan their work carefully. This wastes time and effort.

2 Keep information secure. You must make sure that no one else can get at your work so that:

   a unauthorised people cannot get at confidential information

   b other people do not copy your work and pretend it is their own

   c your work is not lost or damaged deliberately by other people

   d your work is not lost or damaged accidentally.

3 Produce accurate and readable information. Inaccurate and poorly written information will confuse and annoy readers. Also professionally presented information may be believed even though it is inaccurate. This can lead to wrong decisions.

4 Produce work that will be accepted by people or organisations using standard formats – for example your boss at work, and your lecturers, teachers and assessors at school or college.

5 Work safely. Poorly laid out workplaces may cause physical stress or be hazardous to IT operators.

Activity 16

a Give four reasons for keeping information secure.

b Give two reasons why work should be accurate.

Managing your work

The way that you manage your work is important. You *must* be able to:

- plan your work to produce what is required to given **deadlines**
- use the facilities of your IT packages correctly so that you can easily make changes to data
- use file names that are sensible and which help you find your work
- store files so that you can easily find them
- keep a log of any IT problems that you meet, and how you solve them
- check and evaluate your work and suggest how it might be improved.

Planning your work to meet deadlines

Not meeting a deadline makes life difficult for anyone needing your work because if you are late they cannot start theirs on time. Major companies have gone out of business through failure to meet deadlines. You might have failed an exam by missing your revision deadlines, or at least missed a bus by getting up too late.

This course is a preparation for work. If you miss deadlines at work you will find yourself working late, or even be sacked if you persist. If you miss deadlines on this course, your work will be marked down – and you will not gain your GNVQ qualification if you persist in missing deadlines.

Your college or school may have work standards to help you keep to your deadlines. If not, make some of your own. They will stand you in good stead for the rest of your life. You will find some help in managing your work and your time in the Introduction to this book.

Why should you plan your work?

Activity 17

Suggest three ways of planning your work to make sure you meet your deadlines.

Using the facilities of IT packages to make editing easier

It is possible to make a word-processed document look good without using any of the facilities of the package and pretending it is an old-fashioned typewriter. Here are three examples of not using word-processing facilities correctly. You can probably think of many more.

Example 1: 'hard' coding lines

You can use 'hard' coded lines (press the key for a new line at the end of each line) rather than soft ones (let the text flow automatically). Then if you edit a line by adding or removing a word the text can no longer automatically fit itself to the line.

For instance, I recently received an e-mail that looked like this:

```
Hi!>

Can you let me have the e-mail address of your
friend Bernie whom I met at>

your house last week.>

He did give it to me, but I lost the piece of
paper I wrote it on. He uses the>

same music package that I use, and had lots of
good ideas for how to use>

it better.>

Have you finished your assignment for Unit 2 yet?
I am having difficulty with>

the spreadsheet.>

Jo.>
```

Jo had put in her own carriage returns to fit her e-mail page. They did not fit my e-mail page. The hard new line symbol looked like > on my e-mail readout.

Example 2: Lining up columns without using the TAB key

You *can* line up columns of text by pressing the space key several times, like this:

Name	Date of birth	Section
Rita Jones	12/2/60	Computing
Joe Smith	15/3/64	Business Studies
Chris McDonnell	8/12/95	Electronics

However, when you edit the text, the columns will no longer line up:

Name	Date of birth	Section
Rita Jones	12/2/60	Computing
Joseph Smith	15/3/64	Business Studies
Chris McDonnell	8/12/95	Electronics

Using the TAB correctly (instead of the space bar) to line up the columns would have avoided this problem. Changing Joe to Joseph would then not have altered the line-up of the next two columns.

Example 3: Using indents incorrectly
1 Original paragraph:

This is an example paragraph. I am going to indent it half an inch to the right and it will automatically move across the page and the lines will refold themselves correctly. I am doing this by using the indent correctly.

2 Paragraph correctly indented:

> This is an example paragraph. I am going to indent it half an inch to the right and it will automatically move across the page and the lines will refold themselves correctly. I am doing this by using the indent correctly.

3 Indented paragraph edited:

> This is an example paragraph. It is fully justified. I am going to indent it half an inch to the right and it will automatically move across the page and the lines will refold themselves correctly. I am doing this by using the indent correctly.

4 Original paragraph indented incorrectly by using TAB at the start of each line:

> This is an example paragraph. I am going to indent it half an inch to the right and it will automatically move across the page and the lines will refold themselves correctly. I am doing this by using the indent correctly.

(Note that the left-hand side looks all right, but the right-hand side no longer looks justified.)

5 Incorrectly indented paragraph edited:

> This is an example paragraph. It is fully justified. I am going to indent it half an inch   to the right and it will automatically move across the page and the   lines will refold themselves correctly. I am doing this by using the   indent correctly.

(Note that this goes wrong now. The original tabs look like white spaces in odd places.)

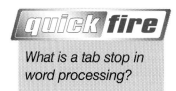

What is a tab stop in word processing?

Use sensible file names which help remind you of the contents

Don't just call your files fred1, fred2 and fred3: you won't remember what they are about. And don't call them letter1, letter2 and letter3 either. It might tell you that they are letters, but not who to, or what about. Give your files names that *mean* something – like joparty (a letter to Jo about a party), u1act1v2 (unit 1, activity 1, version 2). If you use a computer system which does not have a limit to the length of the filename, you can be less cryptic in the name, using unit1activity1version1, etc.

Put the file name in the footer of your file, then if you have printed it out you will know its name. If you also always put the date in the footer, then you won't mix up the latest with a previous version.

Store files where you can find them

If you want to store a lot of papers and be able to find them again, it is

Oh dear! Which one of these is the letter to the builder about mending the roof?

worth dividing them up into groups. You might have stored your schoolwork in different folders, one folder for each subject. If you had two teachers for one subject – geography, for instance – you might have divided your geography folder in half with a piece of cardboard, one half for each teacher.

You can do exactly the same with your disk space or work space on your computer system. You can divide it into separate folders (these are called directories on some computer systems). And you can divide folders (or directories) into sub-folders (sub-directories).

Even better than using u1act1v2 as a file name, create a set of directories (these may be called folders on your computer system) called unit1,

Activity 18

Suggest three ways of storing your work on your computer system so that it is easy to find again.

unit2, etc. Then if you keep all work for Unit 1 in that directory, you won't need the u1 as part of the filename. If you have two lecturers for unit 1, then create a sub-directory of unit 1 for each lecturer. Or you might like to have a separate directory for each activity in Unit 1 – then if you have three versions and two sets of notes for one activity you can use the file names to give you good information about what the file contains.

A possible folder/directory structure

Activity 19

a Design a directory (or folder) structure to meet your needs. Agree the structure with your tutor.

b Create the directories (or folders). Make notes about how to do this.

c Move your existing electronic files into the correct directories and rename them if necessary with sensible names. Make notes about how to do this.

d Print the directory structure. Make notes about how to do this.

Logging your problems

Activity 20

a Find out the procedures for reporting IT problems in your educational establishment.

b Collect copies of any documents used, such as error report forms and fault logs.

c Find out from both the users and the technical staff how well the procedures work

d Design a report about the system for dealing with IT problems in your educational establishment. The design should include

  • probable contents page of the report (what the main sections of the report will be about)

  • layout of the main report

  • layout of the title page.

If you have a computer problem you should *always* make a written note of what the problem was and how you solved it. Write it down in as much detail as possible, with the date and time of the problem. List the following:

1 What program you were using.

2 What stage of the program you were in – i.e. what you have done so far.

3 What was the last thing you did. Write it down keystroke by keystroke.

4 What you were doing when you had the problem. Exactly. Keystroke by keystroke.

5 Write down any error messages you receive exactly.

There are a number of ways to sort out a problem:

1 Sort it out yourself using
   a error messages on the screen
   b the Help menu
   c trying different menu options.

2 Sort it out yourself by using reference material:
   a manuals
   b other books about the program
   c teaching notes from your lecturer.

3 Ask for help from someone near you:
   a another student on the course
   b a student from a more advanced course
   c a technician
   d a teacher or lecturer.

4 Get help from a help desk. This may be:
   a in house, i.e. someone in the college or in a company whose job it is to help IT users
   b from the company that sold you the IT system
   c from the software or hardware manufacturer.

The problem might be that you don't know the program well enough – so try the Help menu. It might not be obvious what to look it up under, so make notes as you go along. Even if you don't find the answer, you might learn other useful things on the way. If you *do* find the answer, write down how you found it – you could need something similar another time.

You may think that you have a software or hardware fault and need to use a telephone helpline. Before using a helpline (especially for a hardware fault) check for obvious mistakes – like whether it is properly plugged in and switched on.

- If possible, ring the helpline while you have the computer running so you can answer all the questions from the other end.
- If you cannot get a phone to the computer it is vital that you have written down the exact details of all error messages and keystrokes – otherwise you will need to ring the helpline several times.
- Make a note of the fix for next time.

Check and evaluate your work

When you have finished a piece of work:

- check it
  - against what you were asked to do
  - for accuracy

- for spelling and grammar
- for how you might improve it
- for layout
- don't make so many corrections that you miss your deadline
- make notes of any improvements you could make in accuracy, information and layout.

Name three checks that you must make before handing in a piece of work.

It can be a good idea to make this check before you start!

Keeping information secure

Protecting information from loss or misuse is *essential* in IT. It is important to

- keep information secure (for example from theft, loss, viruses, fire)
- protect confidentiality (for example, to prevent illegal access to medical or criminal records)
- respect copyright (for example not using or presenting the work of others without permission).

Electronic data can easily be stolen, lost or damaged, so organisations must make a great effort to look after their data. This has to be done physically (keep it safe from theft and fire), electronically (viruses, accidental deletion, unauthorised access), and by law (copyright, data protection act, hacking).

Activity 21

Name three ways that data stored on computer can be lost. How can you guard against each of these?

Physical security

Fire and flood can also damage computers and their data. So can thunderstorms and power cuts.

Locked doors, security alarms and guard dogs can prevent this

Why are back-ups important?

As well as normal security precautions against theft, fire and flood damage, any organisation dependent upon electronic data will need to guard against:

- loss of power – by having their own standby generator
- too much power – by electronically guarding against electrical surges.

More dangers to be prevented

Activity 22

a Discuss what you could do as the manager of a supermarket if your computer system broke down.

b How would you know the value of the goods in the customers' baskets?

c What do you think the customers would do if told to go home without their shopping if they had just spent an hour filling their trolleys?

d Find out from a local supermarket what *they* would do, and how they try to prevent this happening.

Organisations that rely on computers will back up their data regularly, probably at least daily. They should keep back-ups of all their data on the premises, but not in the main computer room. They should also keep back-ups off the premises in case the premises burn down, and will have an arrangement to use other computers if theirs are damaged.

Why shouldn't back-ups be kept in the computer room?

Activity 23

Find out the arrangements for backing up the main computer system in your educational establishment.

Electronic security

Any organisation relying on computer information will have:

Systems to combat computer viruses
Viruses can get onto a computer when loading software and data from disks or over a network, whether a local network or the Internet. They can do great damage to programs and to data. Most PCs will have virus-checking software which runs automatically every time the computer is started up. This should be updated every now and again to guard against new viruses. It is possible to buy software to remove viruses, but it too must be constantly updated. You may have seen reports of viruses affecting large companies in the newspaper or on television.

Back-up systems in case data is lost accidentally
Always keep back-ups of your own work, especially if you share a network with other students. You will have to discuss with your tutor whether you are allowed your own disks at college or school, but you should certainly back up regularly if you have your own computer at home.

Systems of passwords and access rights
Individuals can be given a password and access rights to a system to make sure that they can access the programs and information that they need, but no others.

To stop people who share a network or other computer system from getting at other people's data there should be a way of passwording everybody's own work. A network manager will give everyone certain access rights to the system to allow them to use only the data that they need.

If you have a password system on your college or school computer, it is your job to keep your password secure. If you tell anyone, even your best friend, then you only have yourself to blame if your work is damaged. If you think anyone else has found out your password, change it.

Security law

The Data Protection Act

Private information (such as medical, financial or criminal records) about individuals is confidential. By law, you can not be given information about records other than your own. In fact any data about people held electronically is confidential and the data users must obey the data protection laws of the country.

If your school or college holds confidential data about you electronically, then they must obey the Data Protection Act. You are entitled to see the data that they hold about you, but they can charge you a small fee to cover their costs in showing you.

Sometimes when you fill in a form (when buying something by mail order, for instance) there is a box to tick if you do *not* want your name and address to be passed to other companies. If you do not tick this box, then your name and address can be used by other companies to send you advertisements. Buying and selling mailing lists is big business.

If you work for an organisation that deals with confidential information you will be required to sign a confidentiality agreement in which you promise not to reveal information that you use in your work.

Copyright

Software and data belong to *someone*. If you copy software or data that does not belong to you, then you are stealing. If you buy a computer game, copy it onto your computer and then give the disk to a friend to copy onto their computer you are committing computer piracy. Normally, while you copy the software onto your computer, you are required to agree to the copyright law. Organisations and individuals are heavily fined if they are convicted of infringing copyright.

Are you allowed to scan a picture out of a newspaper to use on a poster?

The copyright law allows individuals and organisations to own the right to any of their work that they have published – whether in printed or electronic form. You are not allowed to use someone else's electronic information (whether program, written work or graphic images) without their permission, for which they may ask you to pay. This rule is the same as for copying printed material.

Software License Agreement

Installing this software constitutes your acceptance of the terms and conditions of the license agreement. Please read the license agreement before installation. Other rules and regulations of installing this software are as follows:

1) The product can not be rented, loaned or leased – You are the sole owner of the product.

2) The customer shall not disclose the results of any benchmark test to any third party without Network Associates' prior written approval.

3) The customer will not publish reviews of the product without prior consent from Network Associates.

4) No liability for consequential damages. In no event shall Network Associates or its suppliers be liable to you for any consequential, special, incidental, or indirect damages of any kind arising out of the delivery, performance, or use of the software. Even if Network Associates has been advised of the possibility of such damages. In no event will Network Associates' liability for any claim, whether in contract, tort, or any other theory of liability, exceed the

A typical software licence. You must agree to it before the software will copy to your computer

/ **Activity 24** /

a Whilst working for the tax office you discover what your friend's father is earning. Are you allowed to tell your friend?

b You have foolishly told your friend your computer password so that you can work on an assignment together. How can you make sure that the rest of your work is secure?

c You borrowed a disk from a friend who now tells you that his computer has a virus. What should you do?

Accuracy and readability

Inaccuracy can mislead and annoy readers.

* Always check your facts – don't tell lies by mistake.
* Make sure proper names are spelt correctly.
* Make sure dates and times are correct.

Many people do not make spelling and grammar checks in informal communications such as memos or e-mail. All possible checks should, however, be made for formal written work such as business letters and reports.

/ **Activity 25** /

a Which of the following faults can be found by using your spell checker?
- I went four a ride.
- I went went by bus.
- I went to the seeside.

b Which of the following faults can be picked up by your grammar checker?
- I are happy in my work.
- are you happy in your work?
- We are all happy with wurking hard.
- The boy said said he was happy.
- I agreed with him..

c What tool could you use to find the readability of a report that you wrote?

d What does readability mean?

e Most grammar checkers suggest you use the active, rather than the passive voice. Which of these sentences uses the active voice?
- I read the book.
- The book was read by me.
- We were robbed by the referee.
- The referee robbed us.

f What does 'print preview' do, and why does it help you design the layout of a document?

g Why do you need to proofread a document by eye as well as use computer tools?

Organisations and standard formats

Organisations often have their own standards for document layouts. This saves time when creating documents as people don't need to think up a layout every time they create a document. It also saves the reader time because he or she will be able to recognise the type of document straight away and know how to act upon it. The following standards are particularly important:

- Business letters present a uniform company style. Readers getting several letters from the same organisation will receive the same company image with each letter.
- Agendas tell people about meetings. If the organisation has a standard format people will remember to put the name of the meeting, the time, date and place and what is to be discussed. They won't forget the date, for instance, and have to send everyone a memo telling them.

- Minutes not only describe what was discussed in a meeting but have a column to say what action is to be taken, and by whom. This reminds the reader of work they must do by the next meeting.

Sometimes letters and reports are proofread by more than one person before being sent out. It is important that everyone uses the same method for correcting mistakes, otherwise no one will understand the corrections made by anyone else. Most organisations use standard proofreading symbols.

Instruction	Mark in text	Mark in margin
Leave unchanged	– – – – – under characters to remain	✓
Insert in text the matter indicated in the margin	⅄	New matter followed by ⅄
Delete	/ through character(s) or ⊢——⊣ through words to be deleted	♂
Delete and close up	⌐ through character or ⊢——⊣ through characters	♂
Substitute character or substitute part of one or more words	/ through character or ⊢——⊣ through word(s)	New character or new word(s)
Set in or change to italic	—— under character(s) to be set or changed	⌐ ⌐
Set in or change to capital letters	═══ under character(s) to be set or changed	═══
Set in or change to bold type	∿∿∿ under character(s) to be set or changed	∿∿∿

Common proofreading symbols for omissions and corrections

Activity 26

a In a business letter, where would you find the name and address of
- the sender
- the recipient?

b What information should go on an agenda?

c Rewrite the following passage correctly:

> *a* Software and date belong to someone. If you copy software or data that does not belong to you, then you are stealing. If you buy a computer game, copy it onto your computer and then give the disc to a friend to copy onto their computer you are committing computer piracy.
>
> Normally, while you copy the software onto your computer, you are required to agree to the to the copyright law. organisations and individuals are heavily fined if caught and convicted. The copywrite law allows individuals and organisations to own right the to any of they're work that they have published whether in printed or electronic form. You are not allowed to use someone else's electronic information whether program, written or Graphic images without their permission, for which they may ask you to pay. This is the same rool as for copying printed material.

Working safely

The main health and safety issues of using IT involve:

- hazards
- bad posture and physical stress
- eye strain.

Hazards

The main hazards of IT equipment are from the electrical fittings:

- cables, plugs and other connections and appliances must be correctly insulated to avoid electric shocks
- cables and equipment must be laid out in such a way as to stop people tripping over them (there are a lot of cables as all the components need to be plugged into each other as well as the mains supply).

What are the three main things to avoid when working in IT?

Physical stress

Sitting badly and having the furniture and equipment badly placed can cause discomfort, leading to physical stress. To avoid this you should have:

- comfortable seating
- a suitable desk and VDU position
- a suitable keyboard position
- brief rest periods at frequent intervals.

Studies have been made of work and its environment, examining the best working conditions for maximum efficiency. These are called ergonomic studies and have resulted in health and safety laws.

The figure shows some of the important features of working with IT equipment. The following should be supplied for an adult of average height:

1 Comfortable eye height above ground is between 1 m and 1.25 m and comfortable viewing distance is between 0.6 m and 0.7 m, so the VDU position should be adjustable.

Ergonomics of working at a computer

2 The keyboard is comfortable at about 0.7 m above the ground. It should be movable separately from the VDU, and its angle of use should be adjustable.

3 A wrist rest should be available.

4 The chair should have an adjustable back rest to support the lower back, and should have no (or low) arm rests to allow maximum arm movement.

5 The height of the chair should be adjustable to allow the user to choose their own height to sit correctly. Comfortable height is about 0.4 m above the ground.

6 The chair should be able to swivel so that the whole body can be moved easily between different activities.

7 The chair should also be movable so that it is easy to get up and sit down and move around the workspace.

8 A foot rest should be available, especially for short people.

9 A minimum distance between seat and table of 0.2 m is needed for knee clearance. As tables are usually of a fixed height (anything up to 0.7 m), it is important that everything else is adjustable.

10 The screen should be away from reflected light, and screened against sunlight. It should also be at right angles to the line of sight. Its position and angle should be adjustable, as should contrast and light and darkness.

11 If data is to be copied in, manuscript holders should be attached to the screen to minimise head movement between screen and documents.

People working at a computer should take frequent short breaks to stretch their muscles. They should be made aware of the risks of repetitive strain injury and should not ignore symptoms of muscular stress.

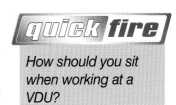

How should you sit when working at a VDU?

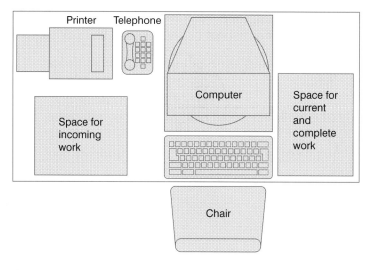

Anyone working at a desk should be able to reach all their work easily. The longest stretches should be for equipment that they use least. A left-handed person will want their equipment arranged differently from a right-handed one

Eye strain

The other problem to look out for is eye strain. Employers of people working with VDUs are required to pay for regular eye tests. It is important to:

Suggest three ways of stopping eye strain.

- avoid long periods of continuous VDU work – vary the work where possible
- occasionally focus the eyes on objects other than the VDU. This will be helped by having a surrounding area that includes objects at various distances for the eyes to focus on.

Activity 27

List the main hazards of working in IT.

Key Terms

After reading this unit you should be able to understand the following words and phrases. If you do not, go back through the Unit and find out, or look them up in the Glossary.

agenda	*fax*
bullet points	*flyer*
business card	*font*
business letter	*footer*
deadline	*grammar checker*
document	*hanging indent*
e-mail	*header*

heading
index
itinerary
layout grid
line spacing
margin
memo
minutes
newsletter
page orientation
page size
readability check
report

screen display
serif
spell checker
subscript
superscript
table of contents
template
text justification
thesaurus
title
tool
wizard

Test Yourself

1 What is the main purpose of a desktop publisher?
2 What package is intended to be used primarily by accountants and mathematicians?
3 Give an example of a document which is sensibly written by hand rather than typed.
4 When giving complex instructions to someone should you
   a use technical terms to make sure the instructions are accurate
   b use language that he or she can understand, or
   c shout so that he or she can hear you?
5 Name and explain two tools on your word-processing package.
6 Name and explain two different tools on your desktop-publishing package.
7 Explain portrait and landscape page orientations.
8 Explain the difference between left justification, right justification and full justification.
9 Explain the difference between a book's contents and its index.
10 Explain copyright.

Assignment for Unit One

You need to produce six original documents that show a range of writing styles and layouts. The documents can be printed, or you can show your assessor on the screen. You must also produce notes describing the documents and comparing two of the documents with three different layouts used by organisations for the same type of document. You must also produce an evaluation of your work.

Get the Grade!

Here are the criteria against which you will be assessed.

To obtain a pass you must ensure that you:

- choose and use appropriate writing styles and layouts so that your documents work as intended
- make appropriate use of page orientation, paragraph formats, line spacing, headings, margins, headers/footers, tabs, bullets, fonts, borders and shading to enhance your documents
- originate suitable information and combine it appropriately with different types of material selected from other sources to create combinations of text, pictures, drawings, charts and tables
- show you can check the accuracy of your work and keep back-up copies of all files
- describe clearly and compare different layouts used by organisations with your own layouts, identify similarities and differences.

To obtain a merit you must also ensure that you:

- make imaginative use of document layouts and presentation techniques to achieve good quality and an appropriate impact in your documents
- show you have proofread your work carefully and corrected obvious errors
- provide relevant explanations for the difference between each of the documents used by different organisations and your own documents
- show you can work independently to produce your work to agreed deadlines
- save and annotate draft work to show clearly the development process for two of your documents.

To obtain a distinction you must also:

- organise different types of information into a convincing and coherent presentation
- ensure that information is accurate and concise and is presented in ways that make it easy to understand
- use technical language fluently and produce clear, coherent and comprehensive explanations and annotations
- provide a constructive evaluation of your documents that identifies good and less good features, suggests possible improvements to them and compares them with standards used by organisations.

For your portfolio

- you might already have enough documents or
- you might be given tasks by your course team.
- Alternatively, you might like to tackle one of the following scenarios.

Help-line

A group activity. You are setting up a business to make life easier for computer users. The ways you can do this are:

- set up the operating systems so that users can get into their favourite programs quickly
- customise application programs so that users have their favourite toolbars, menu settings and defaults
- organise backing up
- set up templates
- set up macros for them
- other useful ideas that you may have.

You will need to:

- organise some market research, such as asking computer users what they would find useful
- decide exactly what help you will offer, and how much you will charge for it
- advertise the business using posters, newsletters and other ideas that you have
- write letters to prospective customers.

You will need to call meetings, for which you will need agendas and minutes to organise the business. You will also need to produce suitable advertisement material, letters, business cards, reports on how to carry out the market research and possibly other types of document.

Charity event

A group activity. You decide to organise a charity event at the end of term. You will need to decide what sort of event to organise and also for which charity. All meetings should have an agenda and minutes should be taken.

Having decided on the event you will need to:

- plan the event and write a report on the plan
- write to people for sponsorship or to invite them to take part

- advertise the event in different ways
- perhaps organise programmes for it
- write instructions to helpers at the event of how to get to the venue
- write one or more press releases about it before the event
- produce other documents that you think are necessary.

Organise an outing

Individual activity. Arrange a trip to an event or place of interest of your choice.

- You will need to write letters to find out the costs for different-sized parties of going to the place or event, and also to find out ways of getting there and back.
- You will need to advertise the outing and arrange a meeting for those interested.
- You will need an agenda for the meeting and will need to take minutes at the meeting.
- You can finalise arrangements according to the response at the meeting and send short newsletters to everyone interested, giving them all the information that they will require for the outing.

Key Skills   *Opportunity*

Communication, level 2	During group work you can show evidence for C2.1a (contribute to a discussion about a straightforward subject).
	You will probably need to read and summarise information from two extended documents about a straightforward subject. One of the documents should include at least one image. You can use this for evidence for C2.2.
	The documents that you produce for this assignment can be used as evidence for C2.3 (write two different types of documents about straightforward subjects). One piece of writing should be an extended document and include at least one image.

Handling information

What is covered in this unit

At the end of this unit you will be asked to produce a relational database and a spreadsheet to meet user needs. You must also produce an evaluation of your work. This unit will guide you through what you need to know in order to successfully put together this work. You will be assessed on this work and awarded a grade, which will be your grade for Unit Two.

Materials you will need to complete this unit:

- a computer system, including printer
- spreadsheet, database and word-processing software
- access to the Internet would be useful
- ideas about presenting information from Unit One.

Introduction

This unit is about handling information. It covers all kinds of information, in computer systems, on paper, in people's heads – everything. Most of the practical work on computers focuses on spreadsheets and databases. This unit will help you to:

- understand what information handling means and how it is used
- create a database to store and use information
- create a spreadsheet to store and calculate numbers
- search, sort, explore and predict new information
- discover trends and patterns from numbers
- work in IT in standard ways and follow good practice

For your portfolio assignment, you will need to set up a solution to a user's problem. This means you will produce a spreadsheet and a database, and write about how your solution works. This assignment is very important, because this is how this unit is graded.

Case study

An example – Hills Road Family Health Clinic

This is an example of the kind of situation in which you use spreadsheets and databases to meet user requirements.

Your client is the manager of a health clinic. Five doctors work there at the moment, and they have around 3000 patients.

They need:

- to track which doctor sees which patient
- to keep medical records on all patients
- to send letters to all patients over the age of 45 reminding them to have a check-up each year.

They also need to manage the finances of the Clinic. Each month expenses like salaries, fuel and petrol costs, and rent for the clinic have to be paid from their income, money from the health authority, which is £4.50 a month for every patient registered with them.

Your clients want to track the income and expenditure of the Clinic every month, showing the result in chart form. They also need to see what would happen if the health authority gave them a different amount per patient.

2.1 Information handling

Information is essential – it is a 'must have'. In our complicated world we could not survive without lots of information. For example you need to know:

- the prices of things in a supermarket so you know which is cheaper, and to make sure you do not run out of money
- the times of trains so you do not miss one
- your bank card PIN so you can withdraw cash from a machine.

To manage a business you need to know what items are selling well. To get a good grade in this course you need a know a lot!

Computer systems can store a lot of **data**. There are different kinds of data – numbers, words, pictures, sounds and so on. When data is put together and given meaning, it becomes information.

Activity 1

A supermarket computer holds this table about the sales of products, and their bar code numbers.

Bar code	Number of items sold
16387	45
19833	72
17832	68
11145	17

Another table contains bar codes and descriptions of the items.

Bar code	Description
17832	Jar of coffee
19833	Packet of tea
18655	Cornflakes
16387	Strawberry jam
11254	Frozen pizza
11145	Bottle of coke

Use this data to find information about what the best selling item is.

Sources of information

These are the places where you find what you need to know. If you are trying to find out something, the first thing to do is to decide what sources of information you can use. Here are six sources of information:

- people – teachers, librarians and other students in your class
- books and directories
- computer databases
- the Internet
- television and radio
- newspapers.

Some sources of information are better than others. When choosing, you should think about:

- how up-to-date the source is – a television news programme will be more up-to-date than a newspaper, and that will be more up to date than a book
- how much information it holds – a newspaper has some, a book has more, the Internet has an enormous amount
- how reliable and accurate it is – the Internet contains a lot of information which is very doubtful – it is often incorrect or sometimes deliberately misleading. Books are more reliable
- how easy it is to search – books often have indexes making it easy to find information, and there are search engines on the Internet. It is often difficult to find topics in newspapers. There is more about this below
- how interactive they are – you can ask a person a question; you can e-mail questions to people on the Internet. Books are not interactive, because you cannot ask them a question in the same way and expect them to give you the answer.

JARGON DRAGON

A *search engine* is something on the Internet that you can use to find information. There are several search engines and they work in different ways, but they all search the millions of sites on the Internet for matching topics, pictures, sounds and so on.

Activity 2

Try to think of six more sources of information you can use. Rate each one according to the above list. Get your teacher to check your answers.

Types of data

There are several different types of data. One example is **text** – words, sentences and so on. A word processor mostly deals with text. Text is made of characters, which are the symbols you find on the keyboard, including punctuation marks and the space character. Examples of text are 'Bill Smith', '12 Acacia Avenue' and '13ExFG'. Even if data contains some numbers (like '12 Acacia Avenue'), it is still text not number. This is because you cannot do arithmetic with it.

Another data type is numbers. The adjective related to this is **numeric** or **numerical**. If some data contains numbers, we say it is numeric or numerical. Numeric data comes in two flavours. Whole numbers are called **integers**. Examples are 5, 324, 17 and –4 (integers can be negative). Other numbers have *decimal fractions* (like 3.45 or 17.01 or –3.33). You might find these referred to as *real numbers* in mathematics books, or *floating point* numbers in computer books. Integers and floating point numbers are stored in different ways in computers. Floating point numbers are slower and not completely accurate.

Much important data is about money, and it is important that calculations about money are completely accurate. Because of this there is a **currency data type**. The unit of currency and the way it is displayed on a computer usually depends on the *country settings* of the machine. Examples of currency data are £34.50 and $2 345.50.

Another data type is date. Much vital information relates to dates – the date of an airline flight, the date of an examination, the date a file was last changed. One problem about dates is that different countries use different formats – for example 03/02/01 means the third of February 2001 in England, but it means the second of March 2001 in the USA – the days and months are the other way around. Date format is usually decided by the computer's country settings.

JARGON DRAGON

Country settings or regional settings on a country let the user set up how currency, numbers, date and time are shown.

Time is another data type related to date. Some software packages include time in a date value. Again, time values can be displayed in different formats – 24 or 12 hour, whether the seconds are displayed and so on. Examples of time values are 9.30 a.m. (using 12 hour clock), or 16:45:30 (using 24 hour clock and including seconds).

Logical data types are not referred to much in everyday life, but they are common in information systems. Logical data is used when the answer can only be yes or no – such as:

- is a person married?
- is a car taxed?
- is a library book on loan?
- is a hotel room vacant?

Logical data (sometimes called Boolean data) is true or false.

Remember – Data types	
• Text	• Date
• Integer	• Time
• Decimal	• Logical
• Currency	

> **Activity 3**
>
> What types are these data values:
>
> * The number of library books someone has out.
> * The speed of a car.
> * Whether a car driver is insured.
> * The date a student joined a college.
> * The fee for enrolling on a course.
> * Someone's surname.

JARGON DRAGON

Data values which are either true or false are often called *Boolean values*. The word comes from George Boole, an Irish mathematician who lived in the nineteenth century and studied logic.

Searching for information

Computers are often used to search for information. Sometimes the searching is done by a person, but to search large sources of information it is faster to use technology. An **index** is a way to speed up searches. Many books have an index at the back, which lists all the topics covered by the book in alphabetical order, so they are easy to find. Next to each topic is the page where the topic is explained.

A **table of contents** also helps to find information. Most books have a table of contents at the front, listing the topics covered, but this time in page number order. This is less easy to use than an index to find a particular topic, but it helps the reader to see how the ideas fit together.

What is the difference between a sort and a search?

Sorting information means to rearrange it so that it is in order. If the information is numeric, it can be sorted into ascending order (smallest number first), or descending order (biggest first). If it is date, it can be sorted into earliest first. If the data is text, it can be put into alphabetical order.

Data is usually sorted because it is then much easier to search.

If you want technology to search for you, you have to 'tell it' clearly what you are looking for. This applies to a single computer searching a database on disk or CD-ROM, or to an Internet search engine. A clear definition of what to search for is called a **query**. Usually a query must be entered in a special language. Some examples of search queries are:

* Find all hotel rooms vacant on 3 July.
* Find all the employees who are married.
* Find owners of cars that are not taxed.
* Find all the library books more than 3 weeks overdue.

Activity 4

a Does this book have a contents page and an index?

b Sort the following numbers into ascending order: 89, 23, 12, 4, 78, 90, 24, 76.

c How can you search the college library for something? Ask the librarian to tell you.

d Find out about search engines on the Internet. Decide which one you like the best, and bookmark it.

JARGON DRAGON

When you *bookmark* a site on the Internet you tell the browser that you like the site and you will want to return to it. The browser stores the address of the site, and it is then quick and easy to pick it out of a list of 'favourite places' on another day.

Data structures

Data structures are ways of organising data. For example, in a newspaper the text is organised into different stories, into columns, paragraphs and sentences. Probably the most important items are on the front page. Information in a television programme is organised so it is clear and entertaining. The information in people's heads is quite often very disorganised!

Data on a computer is often organised into **records**. A record is a set of data items about one thing. For example, a college might keep a record about each student:

Name	Address	Telephone	Date of birth	Gender
Mark Adams	10 Acacia Avenue	01234 5678	15.01.81	M

The record would contain their name, address, telephone number, date of birth, gender, their examination results, what subjects they were studying and so on. Each of these is called a **field**.

A record about a library book would contain fields like title, author, publisher and ISBN. A record about a car would contain fields like make, model, colour, engine size and licence plate number. Most computer databases store information organised into records.

Usually the records are rows in a **table**. The database would have a table containing lots of records like the last one:

> **Remember –
> Searching
> techniques**
>
> - Index
> - Contents
> - Sort
> - Search
> - Query

Name	Address	Telephone	Date of birth	Gender
John Green	1 The High Street	01234 8899	16.02.84	M
Mary May	10b Highrise Villas		01.01.84	F
June Wont	2 Brown Road	01234 5555	25.12.83	F
April Fields	3 Green Avenue		17.05.84	F
Mark Adams	10 Acacia Avenue	01234 5678	15.01.84	M

Most databases contain several tables linked together.

A field

Name	Address	Telephone	Date of birth	Gender
John Green	1 The High Street	01234 8899	16.02.84	M
Mary May	10b Highrise Villas		01.01.84	F
June Wont	2 Brown Road	01234 5555	25.12.83	F
April Fields	3 Green Avenue		17.05.84	F
Mark Adams	10 Acacia Avenue	01234 5678	15.01.84	M

Fields are the columns in a table.

Activity 5

Fill in the gaps using row or column:

- A record is like a . . . in a table.
- A field is like a . . . in a table.

Another common data structure is a *grid*. Grids have *columns* going up and down, and *rows* that go across. Each box in the grid is called a *cell*. You can put grid-like tables of text into a word processor, but most of the text is organised into sentences and paragraphs. Spreadsheets are the key applications that handle data structured as grids. Spreadsheet grid cells can contain text, numbers and formulae, which do calculations.

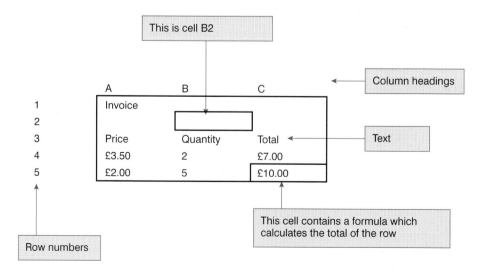

A spreadsheet

Hypertext is the type of structure found on pages on the Internet. The special feature of hypertext is that it contains *links*. Links are usually shown underlined and in a different colour. When the user clicks on a link, they move to another place. The move could be to another place in the same document, or to a different document, or to another page on a different server anywhere in the world.

Dry fly fishing

This means using small flies that float on the water. These are much smaller than lures. Often the fly is treated with 'gunk' that helps it to float on the water. Trout think the dry fly is an insect floating on the water.

Lures

These are fairly big flies. They are often very brightly coloured, and do not look like real flies. They are pulled through the water quickly, and trout will attack them.

Two hyper-linked documents

Hypertext is not just used on the Internet. Many encyclopaedias stored on CD-ROM use hypertext. The links connect words used in one definition to their explanation in another definition. In a similar way, hypertext is often used in on-screen Help files, which help people use applications like spreadsheets.

Remember – Data structures

- Records contain fields
- Databases usually handle records
- Spreadsheets usually handle grids
- Hypertext contains links

2.2 Handling techniques

Different techniques are used to handle hypertext, spreadsheets and databases.

Normal use of hypertext is very easy. An application program called a browser is used to display the hypertext. Using a mouse, the user clicks on a link, and the browser switches to displaying the 'target' that the link points to. If this is being done on the Internet, the browser sends a request to a server to send the new page.

Searching hypertext is not so easy. Most browsers can search for some text, like a word processor can, but this is only *within the page*, and they cannot search other pages which they have not loaded. Searching across hypertext pages is usually done using an index or a search engine.

To create a hypertext document, an application called an HTML editor is usually used. **HTML** stands for hypertext mark-up language. This is a computer language used to code hypertext documents, and is used to do things like set the background colour, the text colour, insert tables and graphics and links. Writing HTML code is like writing a computer program, and some people do this using a simple text editor. However, it is more common to use an HTML editor, because you do not need to know all the HTML codes to use one. This is almost as easy to use as a word processor, and you can quickly see what the hypertext will look like in a browser.

What does HTML stand for?

Database programs handle data organised as tables. Each row in a table is a record, and the columns are called fields. For example, you might set up an 'address book' table that looks like this:

Name	Nickname	Address	Phone number	Email address
John Brown	Johnny	12 High Street Bromley	01243 332211	jb@hotmail.com
Saima Aslam	**Saima**	**221b Brown St. Coventry**	**01203 345543**	**sa@yahoo.com**
Imran Mahmood	Imran	14 Acacia Ave Orpington	0876 254367	imran@csi.com

One record or row

One field or column

Activity 6

Design tables like these for the following databases:

- patient records at a doctor's surgery
- goods for sale in a shop
- sports results
- houses for sale by an estate agent.

Ask your teacher to check your designs

Logical and relational conditions

These ideas are used when selecting records from a database:

- is equal to ($=$)
- is less than ($<$)
- is greater than ($>$)
- is greater than or equal to ($\geq$)
- is less than or equal to ($\leq$)
- AND
- OR
- NOT

The first five of these are used when testing or comparing field values. For example, when using a hotel database to find vacant rooms, the query might be something like:

```
SELECT rooms WHERE vacant = TRUE
```

This would test the field called 'vacant' to find rooms which had this field set to TRUE.

- If we wanted to find rooms that could sleep more than one person, the query could use >:

```
SELECT rooms WHERE beds > 1
```

- If we wanted to find rooms that cost less than £35, we could use <:

```
SELECT rooms WHERE cost < 35
```

- If we wanted to find rooms that could sleep three or more people, we could use ≥ :

```
SELECT rooms WHERE beds ≥ 3
```

- If we wanted rooms that cost £40 or less, we could use ≤ :

```
SELECT rooms WHERE cost ≤ 40
```

AND and OR are used to combine two or more tests. For example, suppose we wanted rooms that cost less than £40 and had a TV – the query could be:

```
SELECT rooms WHERE cost <40 AND tv = TRUE
```

If we wanted rooms that had either a TV or a shower (or both) the query could be:

```
SELECT rooms WHERE TV = TRUE OR shower = TRUE
```

Finally NOT reverses a test. For example, if we wanted rooms that cost not more than £40, we could say:

```
SELECT rooms WHERE NOT cost > 40
```

Activity 7

Can you say NOT cost > 40 in another way, using another comparison you have just seen?

Spreadsheets

Information is stored as tables in spreadsheets, but they are quite different:

- every row in a database table contains the same type of record, but in a spreadsheet different rows can be arranged in a different way – they are not so uniform

- usually some cells in a spreadsheet table contain **formulae**, which calculate a value from other cells.

Here is an example of a small spreadsheet, used to calculate wages:

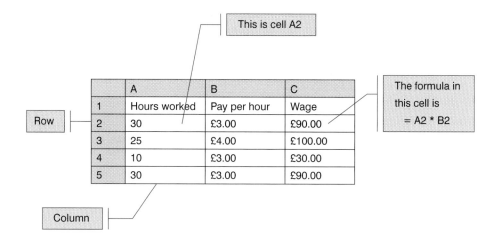

This is cell A2

	A	B	C
1	Hours worked	Pay per hour	Wage
2	30	£3.00	£90.00
3	25	£4.00	£100.00
4	10	£3.00	£30.00
5	30	£3.00	£90.00

Row

Column

The formula in this cell is = A2 * B2

Activity 8

a Referring to the spreadsheet above:
- what is the heading of column A?
- what value is in cell A2?
- what data type is in cell A3?
- what data type is in cell B3?
- what formula is in cell C3?

b Set up this spreadsheet on a computer, save it and print it out.

Spreadsheets have many uses relating to numbers. Common ones are:

- income and expenditure
- sales forecasting
- staff hours, rates of pay and tax
- mortgage payments and interest rates
- material and quantities for jobs
- number statistics.

Spreadsheets are useful for doing calculations. Because they can quickly recalculate new values, they are also used for **'what-if' queries**. This is when the user changes some value (like the price of something or someone's wages) and looks at the new results. This means that a manager can see what would happen if they made some decision, and can help them decide what is the best thing to do. What-if is explained more in the section on spreadsheet methods (page 98).

Spreadsheets can also be used to continue number patterns. This means they can be used to predict or forecast what is likely to happen in the future. For example, a spreadsheet might be used to forecast the profits of a firm for the next year.

Spreadsheets are also able to produce charts and graphs. This is useful because it is often difficult to make sense of a large table of numbers. There might be a pattern or trend in the numbers, but it is not easy to see. Spreadsheets can show the numbers as graphs and charts in a wide variety of forms, such as pie charts, bar charts, line graphs, histograms, three-dimensional graphs and so on. This relates to techniques of presenting information, studied in Unit 1.

2.3 Design of information-handling systems

You might find this topic easier to follow *after* you have worked through the sections on databases and spreadsheets.

An information-handling system is something set up to meet someone's needs. It includes:

* hardware, such as scanners and printers
* software such as spreadsheets
* forms on paper and on the screen
* people and their jobs
* procedures – what happens and when.

This topic covers some aspects of how to design an information system.

Systems are not there for their own sake – they are what someone wants. You design a system for someone, called the 'client' or 'the user.' You set up the system so it does what *they* want. When you design a system, you must follow through the following steps in order:

1 Find out the purpose of the system.
2 Find out what the users want.
3 See what type of information is needed.
4 Work out what processing is needed.
5 Create a storage structure such as a spreadsheet or database.
6 Collect information for storage.
7 Enter and edit the information.
8 Process the information – see below.

For example, the client might be the manager of a sports centre. You would need to talk to this person to discuss what was wanted. For this you would probably have to make an appointment to see the manager, and prepare yourself by planning what you were going to ask. The manager might not be familiar with the idea of information handling, and you would need to help him or her to express clearly in information terms what was wanted. It would help to look at the documents the centre already uses.

Study skills

Interviewing people

Often when you are doing research you need to interview people. Here are some suggestions.

1 Start off with someone in the college – they are likely to be more sympathetic and helpful than someone in another organisation.

2 You might need to telephone the person to arrange the interview. What are you going to say? You should include who you are, why you are calling, when is it convenient for them to see you, date and time and place.

3 Be prepared for the interview – have some questions worked out already. On the other hand do not just read out the questions. Listen very carefully to the answers you get. Make sure you understand them. Ask again if you are not sure. As you get more information, you will think of more questions to ask.

4 You will need to record the information you get so you do not forget. Make quick notes. Do not slow everything down.

5 Do not outstay your welcome! The person will have a lot of their own work to do. At the end, thank them for their time.

6 Try not to be nervous. Most people are pleased to help and like talking about their work.

Once you have clearly identified the user's needs, you need to plan a design using spreadsheets and databases to meet those needs.

In the case of the Sports Centre, the steps in outline might look like the table below:

Step	Outline result
Find out the purpose of the system	Sort out bookings of facilities like the badminton courts
Find out what the users want	Keep track of who the members of the sports centre are, who has booked what and when, and who has paid for what
See what type of information is needed	Names and personal details of the members. Facilities like how many badminton courts there are. Bookings and payments
Work out what processing is needed	Keep a list of members that is easy to check. Book a facility. Check if members have paid
Create a storage structure such as a spreadsheet or database	Use a database table of members. Use a spreadsheet to record bookings for the week
Collect information for storage	Get details of some members, the facilities the centre has, and how much they charge
Enter and edit the information	Put the data into the spreadsheet and database, setting up some imaginary members and facilities
Process the information	Try to make a booking and a payment

Processing data

This really means making the computer use the data to do what you want, such as:

- doing calculations using formulas and functions, probably in a spreadsheet
- sorting the data into order, so it is easier to find
- searching the data, probably in a database
- answering 'what if' questions in a spreadsheet.

Processing like this makes the *computer* find the answer – it does the work for the user. For example, you might search for a person by displaying a table on the screen and looking through the list to find the person. This is no problem if there are 10 or 20 names to look through, but it is not sensible if there are 10 or 20 *thousand* people to search. The idea is that the computer does the searching, not the user.

You also need to design how you want the answer presented. This includes:

- designing the layout of reports, both on the screen and on a printer
- designing graphs and charts if you want the results displayed this way

2.4 Database methods

Remember that databases handle data stored in tables, with one record in each row. For example, a bookshop might keep a table of books.

How many records are there in this table? How many fields?

Title	ISBN	Author	Copies in stock	Price	Bought this week
War and Peace	1–22345–555–6	Leo Tolstoy	2	£14.99	3
GNVQ Intermediate IT	3–44567–345–7	Ann Montgomery-Smith	32	£11.99	36
Pickwick Papers	6–4565–887–X	Charles Dickens	14	£9.99	18
The Water Garden	8–34567–987–0	Philip Swindells	9	£9.75	5
Anna Karenina	4–596587–998–8	Leo Tolstoy	8	£12.49	0
Great Expectations	6–778967–987–X	Charles Dickens	12	£9.99	3
Photoshop in a Nutshell	4–67896–998–3	L. Leclair	5	£12.99	4
Christmas Carol	5–667546–234–9	Charles Dickens	7	£12.67	1

This shows the *data* in the table. If we looked at the *design* of the records in this table, it would look like this:

Field name	Data type	Length	Primary key?
Title	Text	30	
ISBN	Text	13	Yes
Author	Text	40	
Copies in stock	Integer		
Price	Currency		
Bought this week	Integer		

Check through this:

- One *record* is a row in the table
- The *field length* is how many characters long the value can be. In this example, the title can be up to 30 characters long. You can usually only choose the length of text fields. Others, such as integers, have a length fixed by the system.
- The **primary key** is the field that shows which record is which. The primary key should be unique – two rows cannot have the same primary key. In this example, every book has a different ISBN (International Standard Book Number). One author can write two books, but they would have different primary keys.
- The field *data type* is the type of data that can be stored in that column. Choices include text, integer, decimal number, currency, date and logical.
- The *field name* is the title of the column.

Secondary keys

Suppose you wanted to know which books had not sold any copies in the last week – which field would you use as the secondary key?

A **secondary key** is a field which is used to select out certain records, other than the primary key (the primary key is the field used to identify records). In the books table above the primary key is the ISBN, because each different book has a different ISBN. If you were looking for a particular book, you would use the primary key, the ISBN, to find it.

But you might be looking for all the books by Charles Dickens. In this case you would search on the Author field – so you would use Author as a secondary key. Or you might look for all the books costing less than £10.00 – in which case you would use the cost as a secondary key.

Sorting

You have already seen how data can be sorted into order to make it easier to search. For example the books table could be sorted on the author field, so that all the books by Dickens would be together. It would then be easy to find all of the books. What you get is shown in the table below.

Title	ISBN	Author	Copies in stock	Price	Bought this week
GNVQ Intermediate IT	3–44567–345–7	Ann Montgomery-Smith	32	£11.99	36
Pickwick Papers	6–4565–887–X	Charles Dickens	14	£9.99	18
Great Expectations	6–778967–987–X	Charles Dickens	12	£9.99	3
Christmas Carol	5–667546–234–9	Charles Dickens	7	£12.67	1
Photoshop in a Nutshell	4–67896–998–3	L. Leclair	5	£12.99	4
War and Peace	1–22345–555–6	Leo Tolstoy	2	£14.99	3
Anna Karenina	4–596587–998–8	Leo Tolstoy	8	£12.49	0
The Water Garden	8–34567–987–0	Philip Swindells	9	£9.75	5

When a sort is done, it often brings a set of records together – like all the books by Dickens. But that group of all the books by Dickens will still be mixed up – it is in the order Pickwick Papers, Great Expectations, Christmas Carol – so it is not in alphabetical order. If you were looking for a particular book by Dickens, it could still be hard to find. It would be better if you could first sort the books by author, and then get them sorted by title. This is called sorting on multiple fields – a primary field and a secondary field. This is what you get:

Title	ISBN	Author	Copies in stock	Price	Bought this week
GNVQ Intermediate IT	3–44567–345–7	Ann Montgomery-Smith	32	£11.49	36
Christmas Carol	5–667546–234–9	Charles Dickens	7	£12.67	1
Great Expectations	6–778967–987–X	Charles Dickens	12	£9.99	3
Pickwick Papers	6–4565–887–X	Charles Dickens	14	£9.99	18
Photoshop in a Nutshell	4–67896–998–3	L. Leclair	5	£12.99	4
Anna Karenina	4–596587–998–8	Leo Tolstoy	8	£12.49	0
War and Peace	1–22345–555–6	Leo Tolstoy	2	£14.99	3
The Water Garden	8–34567–987–0	Philip Swindells	9	£9.75	5

Now the Dickens books are in alphabetical order.

quick fire

People are listed in the telephone directory sorted by name – but there are a lot of Smiths, Begums and Singhs. Which primary and secondary fields are names sorted by?

Activity 9

a In a database package set up the books table and enter the data.
  - Sort the table into order of price. Use a descending sort, so the most expensive book is first.
  - Sort the table into order of copies in stock, smallest first.
  - How would you sort it to make it easiest to find a particular title?
  - How would you sort it to find the books that were selling best?

b Save the table for use in a later activity.

Searching

Database packages will let the user search a table to find a particular value in a field. For example, you could search the books table for the value 'Christmas Carol' in the Title field.

You can also select a set of records according to some rules. This is called a *query*. The simplest query selects records with a matching value in a field. For example, a query to find all the records with 'Leo Tolstoy' as the author gives this result.

Title	Author	ISBN
Anna Karenina	Leo Tolstoy	4–596587–998–8
War and Peace	Leo Tolstoy	1–22345–555–6

You must be careful when searching text data types, because an exact match is needed. For example, searching for 'LEO TOLSTOY' would give no matches, because it has the author's name in capital letters. Be aware that a query can result in no matches being found.

You can also use the 'less than' symbol, <. For example, if we set up a query for the books that cost less than £12.00 (`price < 12`) the result would be:

Title	Author	ISBN	Price
GNVQ Intermediate IT	Ann Montgomery-Smith	3–44567–345–7	£11.49
Great Expectations	Charles Dickens	6–778967–987–X	£9.99
Pickwick Papers	Charles Dickens	6–4565–887–X	£9.99
The Water Garden	Philip Swindells	8–34567–987–0	£9.75

If we want to find books that cost £11.49 or more, the query would be:

$\text{price} \geq 11.49$ (greater than or equal to 11.49)

This produces:

Title	Author	ISBN	Price
GNVQ Intermediate IT	Ann Montgomery-Smith	3–44567 345 7	£11.49
Christmas Carol	Charles Dickens	5–667546–234–9	£12.67
Photoshop in a Nutshell	L. Leclair	4–67896–998–3	£12.99
Anna Karenina	Leo Tolstoy	4–596587–998–8	£12.49
War and Peace	Leo Tolstoy	1–22345–555–6	£14.99

Sometimes we need to deal with two fields at the same time in a query. For example suppose we want to find books that cost less than £10.00 together with any by Tolstoy. You combine two fields with the words OR and AND. You have to think carefully about this. For example

```
PRICE < 10.00 OR Author = 'Leo Tolstoy'
```

produces this:

Title	Author	ISBN	Price
Great Expectations	Charles Dickens	6–778967–987–9	£9.99
Pickwick Papers	Charles Dickens	6–4565–887–X	£9.99
Anna Karenina	Leo Tolstoy	4–596587–998–8	£12.49
War and Peace	Leo Tolstoy	1–22345–555–6	£14.99
The Water Garden	Philip Swindells	8–34567–987–0	£9.75

But

```
PRICE < 10.00 AND Author = 'Leo Tolstoy'
```

will give you a list of the books by Tolstoy that cost less than £10.00 – and there will be no matches.

You can also use NOT to avoid certain records. Suppose you wanted all books except those written by Tolstoy. The query would be something like

```
NOT (Author = 'Leo Tolstoy')
```

although in some packages you would use

```
Author < > 'Leo Tolstoy'
```

This uses the idea that < > means less than or greater than, in other words not equal to. This gives you all the books *except* those written by Leo Tolstoy, and produces:

Title	Author	ISBN	Price
GNVQ Intermediate IT	Ann Montgomery-Smith	3–44567–345–7	£11.49
Christmas Carol	Charles Dickens	5–667546–234–9	£12.67
Great Expectations	Charles Dickens	6–778967–987–X	£9.99
Pickwick Papers	Charles Dickens	6–4565–887–X	£9.99
Photoshop in a Nutshell	L. Leclair	4–67896–998–3	£12.49
The Water Garden	Philip Swindells	8–34567–987–0	£9.75

Activity 10

Using the table you set up in the last activity, try setting up queries to find:

- All the books by Charles Dickens.
- All the books that cost less than £10.00.
- All the books that have sold more than 10 copies this week.
- All the books written by Charles Dickens or Leo Tolstoy.
- All the books *except* those written by Dickens or Tolstoy.

Designing databases

Often it is a better idea to use *two* tables instead of just one in your database design.

For example, suppose you wanted a system to do stock control in a supermarket. Your first idea might be to have a table about the products for sale. You might think of fields like description, price and number of items you had in stock. What about the key field? You *could* use the description. However, you would want to put a bar-code on the goods so they could be scanned at the checkout, and you would want that to be a number – an integer. The field name could be ID, because that identifies the product. Description would be text, price would be currency, and stock would be integer. The first version of your design might look like this:

ID	Description	Price	Stock
1	Tins of beans	£0.57	10
2	Cornflakes	£1.10	6
3	Jar of Coffee	£0.95	8
4	Bag of flour	£1.24	4
5	Bag of sugar	£1.05	3
6	6 eggs	£0.45	2
7	12 eggs	£0.80	2
8	Packet tea	£1.78	9
9	Cooking oil	£1.89	3

The idea is that when the stock level fell to 0, the manager would order some more. She would probably buy different products from different suppliers. Information about the suppliers would be needed – so the initial design might look like this:

ID	Description	Price	Stock	Supplier	Phone	Address
1	Tins of beans	£0.57	18	NuFood Ltd	01234 556 876	12 Brown Industrial Park Manchester
2	Cornflakes	£1.10	6	RJ Organics	09765 445 667	Sunnyside Farm Devon
3	Jar of Coffee	£0.95	8	Southern Foods PLC	07665 142 453	3 The High Street Bedford
4	Bag of flour	£1.24	4	Southern Foods PLC	07665 142 453	3 The High Street Bedford
5	Bag of sugar	£1.05	3	RJ Organics	09765 445 667	Sunnyside Farm Devon
6	6 eggs	£0.45	2	Southern Foods PLC	07665 142 453	3 The High Street Bedford
7	12 eggs	£0.80	2	RJ Organics	09765 445 667	Sunnyside Farm Devon
8	Packet tea bags	£1.78	9	NuFood Ltd	01234 556 876	12 Brown Industrial Park Manchester
9	Cooking oil	£1.89	8	Southern Foods PLC	07665 142 453	3 The High Street Bedford

NuFood Ltd supply two products, and so their address and phone number is listed twice in the table. Southern Foods PLC supply four items – so their address and phone number appears four times. Clearly this is not a good idea. For example, if Southern Foods changed their phone number, that data would have to be changed four times in the table. It *should* be possible to change it just once.

A better design would be to split this table. The suppliers should be placed in a separate table, listing the suppliers' name, address and other details. Information about the products is kept in the first table.

However, there has to be a link between the tables, so that we know which supplier supplies which product. Also, the supplier table needs a key field, and this can be the link. So know we have two tables – one for products:

ID	Description	Price	Stock	Supplier ID
1	Tins of beans	£0.57	8	1
2	Cornflakes	£1.10	6	2
3	Jar of Coffee	£0.95	8	3
4	Bag of flour	£1.24	4	3
5	Bag of sugar	£1.05	3	2
6	6 eggs	£0.45	2	3
7	12 eggs	£0.80	2	2
8	Packet tea	£1.78	9	1
9	Cooking oil	£1.89	3	3

and one for suppliers:

ID	Name	Phone	Address
1	NuFood Ltd	01234 556 876	12 Brown Industrial Park Manchester
2	RJ Organics	09765 445 667	Sunnyside Farm Devon
3	Southern Foods PLC	07665 142 453	3 The High Street Bedford

How do we know who supplies which items? Look at the bag of sugar – bar code 5. In the SupplierID field, its value is 2 – so it is the supplier with code 2. Look down the supplier table and see that the supplier with code 2 is RJ Organics.

The field SupplierID in the products table is called a **foreign key**, because it matches the ID field in the suppliers table, where it is a key field.

This design is organised and logical. If a supplier's details change (like their phone number), only one value in one table needs to be altered.

Remember – Foreign key

A foreign key in one table is the primary key in another table.

Activity 11

Design a database for an airline, so they know which passenger is flying on which flight. Set it up as follows:

a Design a table of flights. The key field should be flight number. Other fields would be departure airport, destination, take-off date and time.

b Make up just four records in the flight table.

c Design a table for passengers. Use fields like surname, forename and other suitable ones. Include a key field. Also include a field for the flight number. This is a foreign key which links the two tables together.

d Invent data to put 10 records into the passengers table. Make sure there is at least one passenger on every flight.

e Suppose a certain flight was delayed, and the airline needed to phone up all passengers on the flight to warn them. How would they use the two tables to do it?

The link between two tables using a foreign key is called a *relationship* between the two tables. Databases like these, containing tables with relationships between them, are called **relational databases**.

2.5 Spreadsheet methods

Remember that spreadsheets hold data in cells in a grid. Each cell can contain text, numbers or formulae. Every cell has a **cell reference**. For example, cell C5 is in column C and row 5. Some spreadsheets have cell references shown in a different way – for example, R3C4 means row 3 column 4.

The formulae in cells usually use references to calculate values from other cells. For example, the formula in a cell might be = A1 + B4, which means that the value in this cell would be the result of adding cell A1 and cell B4. Spreadsheet formulae use + for add, – for subtract, * for multiply and / for divide. You can also use (brackets) if needed.

Activity 12

Work your way through the following steps using a spreadsheet to create an invoice like the one shown below. Do not try to do it all at once. You will need to check on-line help or the manual, or ask a teacher how to do various things.

	A	B	C	D
1	**Invoice**			
2				
3	Item	Unit price	Quantity	Amount
4	Brass screws	£1.20	7	£8.40
5	Steel bolts	£2.35	4	£9.40
6	Small washers	£0.40	8	£3.20
7				
8		Net Total		£21.00
9		VAT		£3.68
10		Gross Total		£24.68

▶▶

a Put the text and numbers in columns A, B, C and D.
b Increase the width of column A so the text fits.
c Increase the height of row 1.
d Make the text in rows 1 and 3 bold. Make the text in cells B8 to B10 bold.
e Increase the font size of 'Invoice' in cell A1.
f Set the bottom border of A1 and the cells from A3 to D3.
g Format the cells B4 to B6 to display in currency.
h Enter the formulae in column D like this:

Invoice

Item	Unit price	Quantity	Amount
Brass screws	1.2	7	=C4*B4
Steel bolts	2.35	4	=C5*B5
Small washers	0.40	8	=C6*B6
Net Total			=D6+D5+D4
VAT			=D8*0.175
Gross Total			=D9+D8

i Finally, format the numbers in column D to be shown as currency, save and print out the invoice.

Relative cell references

Suppose you wanted a spreadsheet where people could record their expenses like this:

	A	B	C	D	E
1	Expenses				
2					
3	Date	Accommodation	Travel	Other	Total
4	01/06/99	56.6			
5	07/06/99	45.5	15.5		
6	13/06/99		25.5	14.5	
7	19/06/99	134.5	38.5		
8	25/06/99			5.5	
9					

In cell E4 you would need the formula = B4 + C4 + D4

In E5 you want = B5 + C5 + D5

In E6 you want = B6 + C6 + D6

and so on.

The quickest way to do this is to put one formula into E4, and then to copy it down (or 'fill down') into E5 to E8. But notice the formula is not exactly copied unchanged. In every row it is altered so it still refers to the three cells on the left of where it is. This is because it uses **relative cell references.** These refer to cells like '2 cells to the left' or '3 cells down' relative to the current position. This is exactly what is needed in this situation.

Remember – Relative cell references

These change when a formula is copied so they still refer to cells in the same *relative* position.

Absolute references

It is sometimes important to not use relative references – you might need to refer to a fixed cell which does not move when the formula is copied. This is called an **absolute reference**.

For example, the following sheet calculates the amount of VAT on different amounts. The formula in cell B4 is like = A4 * B1. However, when this is copied down column B, the reference to cell B1 has to stay fixed. For example, the formula in cell B5 is like = A5 * B1. The reference to cell B1 is absolute. A way to show this in some spreadsheets is to use B1 – in other words, the formula in cell B4 is *actually*

    = A4 * B1

	A	B	C
1	VAT Rate	17.5	
2			
3	Net	VAT	Gross
4	£0.00	£0.00	£0.00
5	£0.50	£0.09	£0.59
6	£1.00	£0.18	£1.18
7	£1.50	£0.26	£1.76
8	£2.00	£0.35	£2.35
9	£2.50	£0.44	£2.94
10	£3.00	£0.53	£3.53

Remember – Absolute cell references

These do not change when a formula is copied, so they always refer to the same cell.

'What-if' spreadsheets

A 'what-if' spreadsheet is used to find out what will happen if something changes. For example, the manager of a restaurant might want to find out what would happen if he altered the price of meals. At the moment the average price of a meal is £5.50, and it costs about £75.00 each day to run the restaurant. He starts off by setting up a spreadsheet to work out how much profit he would make if different numbers of customers came in. Income is £5.50 per customer. The profit is the income minus the costs. This is the spreadsheet:

	A	B	C
1	average price per meal	£5.50	
2	daily costs	£75.00	
3			
4	No. of customers	Income	Profit
5	2	£11.00	−£64.00
6	4	£22.00	−£53.00
7	6	£33.00	−£42.00
8	8	£44.00	−£31.00
9	10	£55.00	−£20.00
10	12	£66.00	−£9.00
11	14	£77.00	£2.00
12	16	£88.00	£13.00

The formula in cell B5 is = A5 * B1. An absolute reference to cell B1 is used, so it stays correct when copied down column B. In the same sort of way the formula in C5 is = B5 - B2. This shows that he needs to get 14 customers in before he starts to make a profit.

The manager now wants to know what would happen if he raised the menu prices so the average price of a meal were £8.00. He can do this by just changing one number in the spreadsheet – in cell B1. This is what happens:

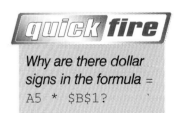

Why are there dollar signs in the formula = A5 * B1?

	A	B	C
1	average price per meal	£8.00	
2	daily costs	£75.00	
3			
4	No. of customers	Income	Profit
5	2	£16.00	−£59.00
6	4	£32.00	−£43.00
7	6	£48.00	−£27.00
8	8	£64.00	−£11.00
9	10	£80.00	£5.00
10	12	£96.00	£21.00
11	14	£112.00	£37.00
12	16	£128.00	£53.00

This shows that he now needs only 10 customers before he starts to make a profit.

Functions

As well as + − * and /, formulae can also use **functions** to do other kinds of information handling. Spreadsheets offer many hundreds of functions – use the help menu to find details of them. Four commonly used functions are SUM, MAXIMUM, MINIMUM and AVERAGE.

For example, here is a spreadsheet used by a teacher to handle students' marks in an examination. On the left is the sheet with actual data, and on the right the formulae.

	A	B
1	**Exam Results**	
2		
3	Student	Mark
4	John	45
5	Jane	67
6	June	32
7	Nadeem	34
8	Ansar	55
9		
10	Average	46.60
11	Best	67.00
12	Worst	32.00

Exam Results	
Student	Mark
John	45
Jane	67
June	32
Nadeem	34
Ansar	55
Average	=AVERAGE(B4:B8)
Best	=MAX(B4:B8)
Worst	=MIN(B4:B8)

Without using a calculator or computer, work out the average of 2, 4 and 9.

These formulae also refer to *regions* of cells – a block of cells together. For example, B4:B8 is all the cells from B4 to B8.

The 'if' function

Spreadsheets can also be set up to do different things in different situations, by testing the values in cells. This is usually done by using an 'if' function. For example, the sheet on page 103 is for someone running a whelk stall in a market. They are charged £22 per day for the stall, and they want to work out how many bags of whelks they need to sell to make a profit. They also want to be able to change the selling price, to see how this would change the situation.

The formula in cell B6 is = A6 * B3. The reference to cell B3 is absolute, so that formula can be copied down. If the selling price in cell B3 is altered, everything is re-calculated.

The formula in cell D6 is = If (C6 > B6, 'Loss', 'Profit'). The if function has three parts. The first part is C6 > B6, which says if the expenses are bigger than the income. The second part is what you get if this is true – a loss. The third part is what you get if it is false – a profit.

	A	B	C	D
1	**Whelk Stall**	**Profit**	**Forecast**	
2				
3	**Selling price**	£0.75		
4				
5	Bags sold	Income	Expenses	Result
6	0	£0.00	£22.00	Loss
7	10	£7.50	£22.00	Loss
8	20	£15.00	£22.00	Loss
9	30	£22.50	£22.00	Profit
10	40	£30.00	£22.00	Profit
11	50	£37.50	£22.00	Profit
12	60	£45.00	£22.00	Profit
13	70	£52.50	£22.00	Profit
14	80	£60.00	£22.00	Profit

The spreadsheet shows that if the price per bag of whelks is 75p, more than 20 bags will have to be sold a day to make a profit.

The stall holder can find out what would happen if they raised the selling price to 90p simply by changing the value in cell B3. This is another example of 'what-if' analysis.

Activity 13

Set up the spreadsheet above. If the stall holder dropped the price to only 50p a bag, how many would they have to sell to make a profit?

Graphs and charts

It is often easier to make sense of numerical information if it is presented in the form of a graph or chart. For example, the following table shows some weather information but it is not easy to see any patterns or trends in this.

Date	Rainfall (mm)	Temperature °C
01/07/99	2	13
02/07/99	4	14
03/07/99	3	14
04/07/99	3	17
05/07/99	0	18
06/07/99	2	19

Showing the information as a line graph makes more sense.

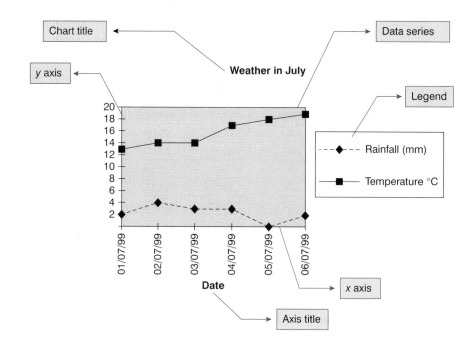

Numerical information is often easier to understand if it is presented graphically

Using graphs also helps the user to see *trends* and *forecast changes* in information. For example, using the last chart, there seems to be a trend of increasing temperature:

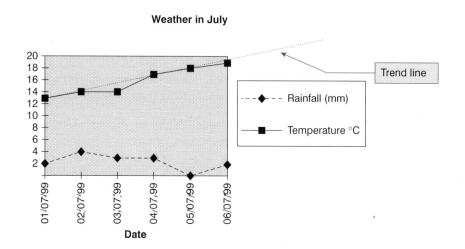

Activity 14

The information in this table is about the New York Stock Exchange. It has been taken off the Internet from http://www.nyse.com. It shows the index (a measure of stock prices) through the start of January 1999. The columns show Composite (an overall figure), Industrial (industrial companies) and Transport (transport companies).

▶▶

Date	Composite	Industrial	Transport
04/01/99	594.12	740.83	475.99
05/01/99	599.91	748.02	485.15
06/01/99	611.01	761.48	502.81
07/01/99	609.19	756.85	501.2
08/01/99	611.06	758.46	506.98
11/01/99	604.04	751.77	496.07
12/01/99	594.59	740.16	482.6
13/01/99	590.72	736.07	475.29
14/01/99	581.07	724.92	470.6
15/01/99	593.39	738.54	477.12
19/01/99	594.83	739.2	477.44
20/01/99	596.09	739.76	471.31
21/01/99	588.03	729.78	468.42
22/01/99	583.75	724.44	461.94
25/01/99	586.06	729.36	465.54
26/01/99	591.45	737	471.09
27/01/99	588.08	735.84	467.42

a Put this data into a spreadsheet and display it as a line graph. Make sure you include a main title, legend and axes titles.

b Try to identify trends in this data – for example, are they increasing or decreasing? By how much each day?

c Once you have seen trends, try to work out what the indexes might have been over the next few days after this.

d Check on the Internet to see how accurate your forecasts were.

Case Study

Financial records – modelling cash flow

Yahoo Line Dancers is a social club of people who like line dancing. They meet every week in a hired room. Everyone who comes to a dance has to pay £4 on the door. Jolene needs to keep track of how much money they have. Every month they have to pay for the room and a band.

The idea of cash flow is:
* they start each month with some money – say £100
* they have to pay for things – say £40
* they receive income on the door – say £30
* so at the end of the month they have £100 – £40 + £30 = £90
* so they start next month with £90.

Jolene records the income and costs for the first six months, and sets up this spreadsheet:

	A	B	C	D	E	F	G
1	**Jolene's Cash Flow**						
2		Jul 99	Aug 99	Sep 99	Oct 99	Nov 99	Dec 99
3	**Opening balance**	£100	£87	£53	£56	£89	£98
4							
5	**Income on the door**	£77	£56	£93	£123	£99	£85
6							
7	**Room Hire**	£40	£40	£40	£40	£40	£40
8	**Cost of Band**	£50	£50	£50	£50	£50	£50
9							
10	**Closing balance**	£87	£53	£56	£89	£98	£93

The formula in cell B10 is

`= B3 + B5 - B7 -B8` (starting amount + income – costs)

and this is copied along row 10.

The formula in cell C3 is

`= B10` (you start one month with what you ended last month with).

By selecting rows 2 and 10 Jolene can create a chart showing the closing balance:

Jolene can forecast the future for Yahoo Line Dancers by:
* setting up more monthly columns
* copying the formulas across in rows 3 and 10
* finding the average of the income on the door, and using that across row 5.

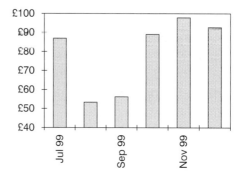

Chart of Jolene's cash flow

If the room hire charge or the cost of the band changes, she can put that in and see how the cash flow is affected.

2.6 Standard ways of working

Unit 1 covered how you should work in an IT situation in depth. These were mostly about

- making sure your work was accurate and had no problems – such as keeping back-ups
- making sure your work was ethical and legal.

You should follow those guidelines in all situations. Here are some points to look out for when you are doing spreadsheet and database work.

- Plan your work to produce what is required. Read portfolio assignments very carefully and make sure you are doing what is needed.
- Plan the timing of your work so it is completed within the deadline. The portfolio assignment will include a date before which it has to be completed.
- Be self-critical. In your portfolio, which parts are good and which are bad? Why? How could you improve your work?
- Make sure the data in your spreadsheets and databases is entered accurately. Read it back and compare it with the original to make sure there are no errors.
- Keep back-up copies of files. If you save your files on a network drive, is it backed up for you? Can you save copies onto floppy disk? You are responsible to making sure your work is not lost.
- Save work in a sensible place, such as on the correct drive and in a folder which makes sense to keep your work organised. Choose filenames that will help you remember which file is which.
- Make sure you do not have a problem with viruses. If you use a computer at home, use up-to-date anti-virus software. Be very careful about anything downloaded from the Internet.
- Respect confidentiality. For the purposes of your portfolio, it is probably best to avoid using any data about named individuals.
- Respect copyright. Do not incorporate any copyright data into your portfolio work. Again you need to be very careful with data from CD-ROMs or the Internet.

Keep it safe and legal

Check planning, deadlines, accuracy, back-ups, viruses, confidentiality and copyright.

Key Terms

After reading this unit you should be able to understand the following words and phrases. If you do not, go back through the unit and find out, or look them up in the Glossary.

absolute reference	numerical
cell reference	primary key
currency data type	query
data	records
fields	relational database
foreign key	relative reference
formula	secondary key
functions	sorting
HTML	table of contents
hypertext	tables
information	text data type
integers	what-if query
logical data type	

Test Yourself

1 Name four sources of information.
2 Text is one type of data. Name three more.
3 What is the difference between a sort and a search?
4 What are the missing words – A record is a . . . in a table. A field is a . . . In a table.
5 What is hypertext?
6 Make up an example of 'what-if' with a spreadsheet.
7 What does the primary key of a table mean?
8 What is a foreign key?
9 What is the difference between relative and absolute cell references?
10 Name three functions you might use in a spreadsheet formula.

Assignment for Unit Two

You need to produce a relational database and a spreadsheet to meet user needs. These must include a description of the system and annotated printed output demonstrating its operation and showing how it meets user needs. You must also produce an evaluation of your work.

In other words, you have to set up a spreadsheet and a database to do what someone wants. You have to write about how it works. 'Annotated printed output' means that you prove it works by printing it out, and you must add notes explaining what each print-out shows. You also have to write about how good you think your work is.

Get the Grade!

Here are the criteria against which you will be assessed.

To obtain a pass you must ensure that you:

- describe clearly the user's needs, the information to be processed and the processing required
- create table structures using suitable field names, field lengths, data types, primary keys, relationships and sort and search criteria
- create and use suitable spreadsheet row heights, column widths, cell formats, titles, cell references, IF. . .THEN statements, arithmetic functions and formulae
- use your data-processing skills to enter data, sort, search, calculate, predict results, produce different types of charts or line graphs and create printed reports using related tables
- produce printed copy showing that you have met the above requirements and explaining your work (this may include screen prints or annotated data output)
- show you can check the accuracy of your data and keep back-up copies of all files.

To obtain a merit you must also ensure that you:

- use software effectively to sort on multiple keys, make use of cell relationships and produce good quality printed copy, showing data content, formats and formulae (clear and detailed annotation, screen prints or notes must explain why and how all printed items are produced)
- make good use of titles, graphic lines, spacing, text size, text enhancement, column and row headers, page headers or footers and graph labels to enhance the presentations, making them easy to read and free of layout errors
- show you have checked your work for accuracy and correct obvious errors
- show you can work independently to produce your work to agreed deadlines by carrying out your work plans effectively
- organise your work so that it shows clearly how it progresses from the design stage to completion and evaluation.

To obtain a distinction you must also ensure that you:

- show an in-depth understanding of database and spreadsheet systems and evaluate your work to make suggestions for improvement and to describe any problems experienced
- use technical language fluently and produce clear, coherent and comprehensive explanations and annotations
- make effective and efficient use of complex search criteria on related tables, formulae and absolute cell references to produce the desired outcomes.

For your assignment, you might be given a task by your course team. This might be an imaginary scenario, or it may be a real system and you may have to interview users. Alternatively you could do the Hills Road Health Clinic task described at the start of this unit, or tackle one of the following scenarios.

West Midlands Sunday Football League

Bill Jones is the secretary of the West Midlands Sunday Football League. There are about 10 teams and 200 players. Players have to be registered with the League and pay a fee of £20 per year. The League has to pay a £30 pitch fee for every match played.

Bill needs:

- to keep records of player and team details, including who plays for which team
- to print an alphabetical list of players for each team
- to send letters to players who have not paid their annual fee
- to record the number of points won by each team
- to print out the league table
- to keep track of how much money the League has, and to report this as chart on a month-by-month basis.

At the end of each season there is a party at a room in a hotel which Bill hires. The hotel charges £100 for the room, plus an amount per head depending on what type of food they have. Bill needs to work out how much to charge each person who comes, estimating how many people might want to come.

Val's Videos

Val likes old films, and she records them off the television onto video. She has around 100 videos. Most tapes have 6 hours total playing time, and so she can record two or three films on each tape.

Val wants to:

- know which films she has, including the title, the stars and what type of film it is
- know which film is on which tape
- use the tapes efficiently, so she wants to know how long a blank section there is left on each tape
- be able to find films with particular stars or certain types of films.

Val's day job is working in marketing for a film distribution company. She has to get information on the weekly box-office receipts of new films, so that she can report on the most popular films each week, and produce charts showing how popular a certain film is week by week.

Art Gallery – paintings and artists

Sharon is the manager of a large art gallery. They have about 300 paintings by nineteenth and twentieth-century artists. She has to deal with the finances of the gallery. Each month there are regular costs like salaries, fuel, advertising and the purchase of new paintings. Income comes from entrance fees (£4.50 a head) and sales from a shop of goods like posters and books.

She wants to be able to:

- keep track of the details of the paintings they have
- print a list of all the paintings by a certain artist
- print a list of the paintings on a room-by-room basis
- handle the cleaning of paintings – each one is cleaned every 3 years, and she needs to know which ones are due to be cleaned
- track how much money the gallery has, and produce line graphs of income and expenditure each month.

Key Skills — **Opportunity**

Application of Number	When you use information sources, you will have an opportunity to interpret information from two different sources, including material containing a graph (N2.1).
	When you use spreadsheets, you will have an opportunity to carry out calculations (N2.2) to do with:
	• amounts and sizes • scales and proportion • handling statistics • using formulae.
	When you produce charts, you will have an opportunity to interpret the results of your calculations and present your findings (N2.3). You must use at least one graph, one chart and one diagram
Communications	When you try to identify users' needs and plan solutions, you will have an opportunity to:
	• contribute to a discussion about a straightforward subject (C2.1a) • give a short talk about a straightforward subject, using an image (C2.1b). ▶▶

If the user provides information on paper, you will have an opportunity to read and summarise information from two extended documents about a straightforward subject (C2.2). One of the documents should include at least one image.

When you write a description of the system and evaluate your work, you will have an opportunity to write two different types of documents about straightforward subjects (C2.3). One piece of writing should be an extended document and include at least one image.

Hardware and software

What is covered in this unit

3.1 **Hardware**
3.2 **Software**
3.3 **Computer programming**
3.4 **Macro programs**
3.5 **HTML programs**
3.6 **Standard ways of working**

At the end of this unit you will be asked to set up a computer system for a user. This will include producing templates, macros and HTML pages according to the user's needs. This unit will guide you through the skills you will need to successfully put together this work. You will be assessed on this work and awarded a grade, and this will be your grade for the unit.

Materials you will need to complete this unit:

- a computer with printer and Internet access
- word-processing software which lets you set up templates
- spreadsheets with macros available
- a web browser
- an HTML editor.

Introduction

This unit is about setting up computers so that users can make best use of them. The following areas will be covered:

- How users can be helped to pick out the details of a computer system which would best suit them – an IT **specification**.
- Choosing computer parts to meet a specification, and setting them up the best way – setting the system **configuration**.
- Writing small programs (**macros**) which let users work more efficiently.
- Creating **hypertext** documents similar to those seen on the Internet – **HTML**.
- Understanding and developing good practice in your use of IT.

The unit uses ideas from Unit 1 on presenting information, especially experience of word processing and desktop publishing, where you looked at the use of templates. It also builds on Unit 2, leading to hypertext and macros.

JARGON DRAGON

A *specification* is a short description of what a system is made of or what it can do. For example, a computer specification would say how much memory it has, what kind of disk drives, what kind of printer and so on.

As you work through the unit, you will learn the ideas and develop the skills needed to complete the assignment.

This unit includes a portfolio assignment. If you look at the end of the unit you will see that the assignment is a practical task about setting up computers so that users can make best use of them.

3.1 Hardware

The parts of a computer made of actual equipment are called the **hardware**. If you can touch it, it is hardware. Examples of pieces of hardware are keyboards, mice and VDUs.

The user controls what a computer does by making use of the various programs in the system. **Software** means the programs in a computer. Software is made of a set of instructions to the computer telling it what to do. The instructions are coded, and are stored on disk or in memory. You can touch hardware but not software.

There are four kinds of hardware items:

- input – such as keyboard or mouse
- processing – such as memory, micro-processor chips (like the Pentium)

- output – such as VDU and printer
- file storage – such as disk drives.

This list reflects how computers are used.

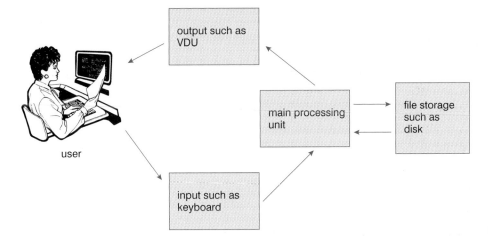

How computers are used

JARGON DRAGON

A *VDU* is a visual display unit – it is also called a monitor, a screen or a display.

Remember – Hardware and software

- Software means programs
- Hardware means physical equipment

Amounts of information

The arrows in the figure above show how information flows between the different parts of the system.

Taking notes

This section contains a lot of facts, which you must learn. One way to help you remember material is to make notes on it. Here are some suggestions:

- Make sure you have a folder to carry your work in.
- Organise those notes into different sections for different teachers or different units.
- Use clear headings, underlined, to structure your notes.
- Use your own words – do not just copy.
- Use diagrams.
- Keep it as neat as possible.

All information in a computer system is binary – which means it is coded as a set of zeros and ones. A **bit** is a 0 or a 1 – a binary digit. All data in a computer system is made out of bits – text, images, sounds, software, control signals, numbers and everything else. All data is stored in the form of binary patterns. A **byte** is a group of eight bits. Usually a byte can code one character. An integer is usually stored in two, four or eight bytes.

JARGON DRAGON

A *character* is one of the symbols on a keyboard, such as a letter of the alphabet or a punctuation mark. An *integer* is a whole number.

Bits and bytes are very small amounts of information. Thousands or millions of bytes are needed to store documents or graphics, and so there are words for larger amounts of information.

A **kilobyte** is about 1000 bytes. The usual abbreviation for a kilobyte is kB. One page of text is about 1 kB. A small graphic image might be 50 or 100 kB. A **megabyte** is about 1000 kB or 1 000 000 bytes – a million bytes, abbreviated to MB. A medium-sized graphic might be 1 MB. One floppy disk usually holds between 1 and 2 MB. The memory of an average computer is around 64 MB. A **gigabyte** is about 1000 MB, abbreviated to GB. An average hard disk holds about 5 GB. A **terabyte** is about 1000 GB, abbreviated to TB.

quick fire

How many bits in a byte?

quick fire

About how many pages of text could you store on one floppy disk?

Remember – Bits and bytes	
• A bit is a 0 or 1	• A byte is 8 bits

Input hardware

There are many types of input device. You need to be able to choose the correct device to meet the needs of users, because each one is best for a different job. Here are the most common input devices.

- Keyboard – the standard keyboard as found on standard PCs. Keyboards are used for inputting text to produce word-processed documents, e-mail, or enter data into a database.

The concept keyboard has many different uses. Here a technician is using a concept keyboard to help control the Burgon oil field in Kuwait

- Concept pad (plastic film keyboard). These have a small number of areas which can be pressed. Each area is covered by a picture or symbol. The areas are fairly large, so no manual dexterity is needed, and they are very robust. They are used by small children who cannot read, or disabled people. They are also used in systems in public areas, such as timetable displays in bus stations, because they are very hard-wearing.
- Mouse – used for input in a **GUI**, selecting items from a menu or links in **hypertext**, and creating graphics.
- Roller ball – sometimes called a tracker ball. This is effectively an 'upside-down mouse' but unlike a mouse it does not need a desk area to work on, so it is often used in lap-top computers.
- Joystick – like a gear stick on a car or a joystick in an aircraft. Because they can signal 'up, down left or right' joysticks are often used in games systems, or to control machinery.
- Scanner – a graphics scanner can read in a text document or graphic on paper. Don't confuse a graphics scanner with a bar-code scanner, which can only read a bar-code.
- Digital camera – like a traditional camera except that it has a photo-electronic screen in place of the photographic film, and the pictures are stored in the camera's memory until they are transferred through a cable into the computer.

A joystick

117

- Microphone – connected through a sound card into the computer. Used for music recording, voice messages, or in speech recognition systems where the user speaks their commands to the computer.

JARGON DRAGON

GUI stand for graphical user interface – such as Windows, where the user sees and uses small pictures and windows on the screen. The alternative is a 'character-based interface', where the user has to type in commands in a special language.

Activity 1

Which input devices would you recommend for the following users:

a A disabled person with limited use of their fingers.
b A disabled person with no use of their fingers.
c A newspaper photographer.
d Someone controlling a crane using a computer.

Output devices

There is a variety of output devices, which must be selected to meet the requirements of the user. Three common types of devices are VDUs, speakers and printers. You need to be able to understand the technical terms used with each.

Visual display unit

These are also called VDUs, monitors or displays. Most VDUs are based on cathode-ray tubes (CRTs), as used in televisions, but some are flat-panel devices based on plasma discharge or liquid crystal displays, most commonly used on a lap-top where a CRT is impossible.

The size of a VDU is measured from corner to corner. The measurement should be across the actual viewing area, but sometimes it is taken to include the border surrounding the screen, so that the size of the screen is less than might be thought. VDUs vary in size, the most common being 15 inches. Larger VDUs are 17 inch or 21 inch. These are much more expensive, but provide a much better display, so they are used where graphics is the main purpose of the system.

Displays that show only one colour against a black background are called **monochrome**. These are usually green, amber or white. In the early days nearly all displays were monochrome, and colour VDUs were much more expensive. Now most are colour. Note that in many computer manuals you will see colour spelt color, the American version.

Computer displays are made of rows and columns of tiny dots, or **pixels**. Pixel stands for *pic*ture *el*ement – one of the dots making the image. The number of pixels across and down a display is its **resolution**. For example, the resolution might be 640 × 480, which means there are 640 pixels across the screen and 480 down it. A higher resolution means more pixels, smaller pixels and a better display. There are some standards for screen resolutions and the number of colours which can be shown. Examples of these are CGA, VGA and SVGA. How good the display looks is actually a combination of

- the **video card** in the system (this is a printed circuit board in the main processing unit, connecting the motherboard to the display)
- the **display driver** in use (this is a piece of software used to control the video card). Each different video card has its own driver, and this needs to be used to use the maximum power of the card
- the VDU which is being used. A high-resolution video card will not produce a good display unless it is connected to a high-resolution VDU.

Another issue concerning VDUs is their **refresh rate**. The image is drawn on the screen by a spot which scans across a line on the top of the screen, then the line beneath it, then the next and so on down to the bottom of the screen. This completes the image, and then the scan starts again. The refresh rate is how many times the screen is scanned every second – 25, 50, 80 or more times per second. A low refresh rate produces a picture which flickers slightly, and this can cause headaches and eye strain after prolonged use.

Some VDUs draw every second line in one scan, then the lines in between in the next scan. This is called an **interlaced display**. An interlaced display can also produce a flickering image and cause eye strain, which is avoided by using a non-interlaced VDU.

Printers

Printers are used in many different ways. For example:

- printing receipts at a supermarket checkout
- a student may use a printer at home to do course-work and print 10 or 20 pages a week
- a printer may be shared between 10 workers on an office network – producing 5000 pages per week
- to produce electricity bills for customers – half a million bills every 3 months
- producing photographic-quality colour prints in a graphics department – 50 pages a week.

What is a monochrome VDU?

What does resolution mean?

What is a pixel?

What's so good about a high refresh rate?

Remember – Display terms

- Pixel
- Resolution
- Monochrome
- Refresh rate
- Interlace
- Video card
- Display driver

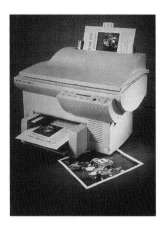

An ink-jet printer

How does an impact
printer work?

Different kinds of printers work in different ways, and that makes them suited to different kinds of tasks. An **impact printer** works by hammering pins or embossed letters through an ink ribbon onto paper. These are often cheap, and they are essential if multi-part stationery is being used because more than one copy of the print-out is needed. For example, if a business is printing out a purchase order for goods from a supplier, they will post the top copy to the supplier, and keep the second copy on file.

Probably the most common type of printer in general use is an **ink-jet printer**. This works by firing a stream of tiny droplets of liquid ink onto the paper. The droplets are given an electrical charge, and can be deflected to form the shapes of the letters or graphics. By using cartridges containing ink of several colours, colour printing can be obtained. Ink-jet printers can provide good-quality colour printing fairly cheaply, which is why they are so common.

Laser printers were developed from photocopiers, and they work in a similar way:

1   The image to be printed is sent from the computer and controls a laser firing onto a drum. This controls a charge of static electricity on the drum. The electrical charge is higher where the image should be darker. This charge attracts toner powder onto the drum, in the pattern of the image to be printed.
2   The drum rotates and moves near the paper. A wire gives the paper an electrical charge opposite to that on the drum.
3   Because of the opposite charges, toner is attracted from the drum onto the paper, still in the pattern of the image.
4   The paper is heated, which 'fuses' the toner permanently onto the paper.

Laser printers can be very high quality and fast. Colour lasers are also available, but are very expensive.

The idea of **printer resolution** is the same as for the resolution of an image on a VDU – it means how small the dots are, or how sharp the image is. It is usually measured as 'dots per inch' or dpi. A typical value is 600 dpi. This would be fine for printing ordinary text, but a printer that was intended to print out the highest quality colour images of photographic standard would need more than this.

Other considerations in choosing a printer:

• How fast it is – how many pages it can print per minute. For a single user printing one- or two-page letters this does not matter much, but if long documents are printed, or if it is a network printer being shared by many users, high speed is important.
• How much paper it can hold. A large mail merge, for example, might print out many hundreds of sheets of paper, and it is much more convenient if this can be done without having to refill the printer.

- How robust and hard-wearing it is. A printer for home use will not be heavily used, whereas a network printer will print thousands of pages every week.
- The cost of replacement toner cartridges. These can be one-third or more of the total cost of the printer.

Activity 2

What type of printer would you suggest for:

- A student doing course-work on their computer at home?
- Printing receipts at a petrol station?
- A marketing department producing designs for posters?

Remember – Printers

- Impact
- Ink-jet
- Laser

Speakers

Speakers or loudspeakers are connected to a computer through a sound card and produce sound output. They are useful for:

- music technology applications, where music is created using a computer
- multi-media applications, where material is presented in the form of video and sound for education or entertainment
- situations where the user cannot look at a VDU – for example if they are disabled, or a surgeon performing an operation.

Main processing unit

The input and output devices are connected to the main processing unit – the actual 'computer'. This contains a power supply unit, **motherboard**, interface cards and file storage devices, described in the following sections.

The **central processing unit** or **CPU** is usually a single integrated circuit – a **micro-processor**. There are several 'families' of microprocessor, such as the x86 series from Intel which includes the Pentium, the 68000 series from Motorola used in Macintosh computers, the PowerPC and Alpha processors. A microprocessor is the 'heart' or the 'engine' of the computer. It can carry out program instructions by doing arithmetic and logic. Modern microprocessors are *very* fast – typical clock speeds are around 500 MHz.

A micro-processor chip

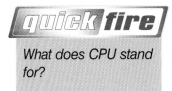

What does CPU stand for?

JARGON DRAGON

Clock speed measures how fast the electronic clock inside the processor works. This is measured in megahertz, abbreviated to MHz. 500 MHz means 500 million 'ticks per second'.

The **memory** of the computer is made of **integrated circuits**. The memory stores programs while they are running, and holds data the programs are using. A typical computer will be able to store 64 MB of data in memory. If a computer has more memory, it can run more programs at the same time, run bigger programs, produce higher resolution graphics – and it will run faster because it does not have to keep extra data on disk, which is relatively slow.

What is the difference between ROM and RAM?

There are two basic kinds of memory. **ROM** (read-only memory) is permanent and cannot be changed – data can be read out of it, but new data cannot be written into it. ROM is used, for example, to store the programs the computer runs when it is first switched on, such as a memory test and loading the **operating system**.

The other type of memory is **RAM**, which stands for random-access memory. The special thing about RAM is that new data *can* be written into it. RAM is used to hold programs such as word processors while they are running – they are held in files on disk when they are not in use. RAM also holds graphics data which is displayed on the screen.

An **interface card** is used to connect other devices to the computer. Examples are video cards which connect to the VDU, network cards which connect to a LAN, sound cards connecting to a microphone and speaker. Another card might be a modem, which can be used to connect the computer through a telephone line to the Internet. Older computers often have one interface card that connects the keyboard, mouse, floppy and hard disk drives, while more recent machines have these interfaces directly on the motherboard. An interface card will have a port to which the device is connected.

A video card

JARGON DRAGON

A set of computers in one room or building that is linked together so they can exchange data is a *LAN*.

A *port* is a place for a cable to be connected to a computer, for either input or output. For example, a printer would be connected to a printer port.

The motherboard is a large printed circuit board, upon which is placed the CPU and memory chips. These are connected together by a **bus**, which also connects to the interface cards. A bus is a 'data highway' – it is a set of wires along which digital data is sent. The bus is used to send data between the CPU, the memory and interface cards.

What things are connected to the bus?

The **power supply unit** (PSU) connects to the mains electrical power, and changes it to low-voltage power suitable for the other devices in the processing unit.

When the computer is switched off, most of the information held in memory is lost. This is because most memory is **volatile** – the data is lost when the power is off. Normal RAM is volatile, so work has to be 'saved' onto disk if it will be needed again. ROM is non-volatile, so the data in it is ready as soon as the computer is switched on.

The CPU contains an electronic clock that controls the speed at which it works. Clock speeds are measured in megahertz, abbreviated to MHz. 1 MHz is one million 'ticks' per second. Typical clock speeds are currently around 500 MHz – 500 million steps every second.

Memory chips are not as fast as the CPU, but they are still very fast – much faster than disk drives.

What is a PSU?

Where would you find the CPU chip?

Activity 3

How much memory do your college computers have? Which CPU do they have? What is their clock speed? What interface cards do they have?

Remember – ROM and RAM

- ROM is read-only memory – the data in it cannot be changed
- Data in RAM *can* be changed

File storage devices

Because RAM is volatile, we need a way to permanently store work, or everything would be lost when the computer was switched off. This is usually done by saving work in files on different kinds of disks – magnetically on floppy or hard or other disk, or optically on CD-ROMs or DVDs.

Floppy disk drives

Most floppy disks hold 1.44 MB of data. Floppies are slow to read and write, and not very reliable. They are mostly used to transfer small files between computers. Floppies can normally be written to as well as read from, but they have a small notch that can be opened to make them read only. This gives some protection if the data on the disk is important. Floppy disks are removable – they can be taken out of the drive very easily.

Hard disk drives

Hard disk drives are faster than floppies, are more reliable, and hold much more data. Average capacity is around 5 GB – the same as around

Hard disk drive with the cover removed

5000 floppy disks. Hard disks are read and write, but are not normally removable – you cannot take a hard disk out of a computer without dismantling it.

Optical storage – CD-ROM and DVD

CD-ROM and DVD discs are made of sheets of aluminium covered with clear protective layers of acrylic. Very tiny pits in the aluminium are used to code the binary data.

CD-ROMs are older than DVDs. They hold about 700 MB of data. The first CD-ROM drives were slow, but the current versions run 36 times faster. CD-ROMs are usually read only – they are bought with data on them, and they cannot be changed. However it is also possible to buy:

- recordable CDs, where you buy a blank CD and, using a suitable drive, write data onto it, after which it is read only and cannot be changed
- rewritable CDs, which can be written to many times like a hard disk, but slower.

DVDs look like CDs but use a different format so that more data can be stored on them. This enables full-length movies with video and sound to be stored on a single DVD disc. The standards for DVD are still developing.

Other types of drive

Standard floppy disks can hold only 1.44 MB, and this is too small to hold many files, especially graphics. Because of this there are now a range of other types of drive with higher capacity – such as Zip drives and Bernoulli disks.

Activity 4

Search through computing magazines and make a list of:

a Motherboards with different processors and clock speeds, and their prices.
b The prices for RAM.
c Different kinds of printers and their prices.
d Prices of floppy drives, hard drives of different capacities, CD drives and DVD.
e VDUs of different sizes with prices.
f Prices of different network, sound and modem cards.

Study Skills

Sources of information

Sometimes you need to find out information for yourself. Sources you can use include books from the library, magazines, newspapers, videos, CD-ROMs, the Internet, other students, other teachers, other experts. But check that:

* you acknowledge the source in your work – say *exactly* where you got the information from
* the information is relevant – that it is actually about what you want
* it is up-to-date
* it is reliable, valid and true – much of the material in magazines or the Internet is just the opinion of one person, and should not be relied on.

3.2 Software

Software means programs. Computer programs are made of instructions coded in special languages. Software is normally stored on disk, and is loaded into memory when it is running. The instructions in the program then control what the computer does.

Here are some examples of pieces of software:

* word processors such as Word, WordStar and Word Perfect
* spreadsheets such as Excel and Lotus 1-2-3
* databases such as Access, dBase and Paradox
* graphics programs like Adobe PhotoShop and Corel Draw
* DTP like PageMaker, Page Plus, QuarkXPress
* financial software like Sage and Pegasus
* communications software such as Eudora, Netscape Navigator and Internet Explorer

- operating systems like Windows 95, Windows NT and Linux
- utilities like Norton anti-virus software
- drivers for video cards, network cards or printers
- programming systems, such as Visual Basic.

JARGON DRAGON

A *computer virus* is a small program which is intended to cause harm or be a nuisance to a computer system. A virus tries to hide itself, and copy itself from one machine to another – usually via floppy disks or networks.

Software that basically makes the computer work is the **system software**. Examples are operating systems, anti-virus software, communications software and printer drivers. Without the system software the computer would not work. System software is about computers. However, if you only had system software, you would not be able to do anything useful with your computer.

The software that allows you to do things like calculate wages, control stock, produce music CDs, keep lists of your friends with their names addresses and phone numbers, is called the **application software**. These software items are called applications. They let you apply your computer to do useful things in the real world. Applications need system software to make the computer work, but they then do specialist tasks to do something useful.

quick fire

What is system software?

Graphics and drawing programmes are application programmes

Software like word processors, spreadsheets and databases are general tools, but they can be set up to do specialised tasks. Because of this they are sometimes called *generic* applications. For example, a spreadsheet program (like Excel) will not calculate wages – but a spreadsheet can be set up which will.

For this unit, you need to learn how to use some pieces of system software so that you can configure computer systems to meet users' needs.

Software in ROM and system settings

Remember that there is some software in the computer's ROM, which runs when the computer is first switched on. This system software will do things like check the RAM and then start to boot the operating system.

JARGON DRAGON

Booting is what happens when a computer starts up, and the operating system software is loaded from disk into memory and started.

Other parts of ROM will contain the **BIOS** – the Basic Input Output System. The BIOS contains small pieces of program which can do things like reading a key pressed on the keyboard and displaying a character on the screen – in other words, basic input and output. Without the BIOS, the computer cannot be used at all.

The computer also has a small amount of special memory, called CMOS-RAM, which is powered by a small battery. This stores some settings of the computer which need to be kept, but which might need to be changed – they cannot be in ROM – for example which drives to try to boot from. When a computer is switched on, it will often first try to boot from a floppy disk, and then if it cannot find one, it will boot from a hard disk. This means that if the hard disk develops a fault you can still boot from a floppy. However, this risks virus infection, if the machine is switched on with an infected floppy accidentally left in the drive.

The CMOS settings can be altered by pressing a key when the machine powers up. To stop people 'meddling', this is usually protected by a password.

Remember – Software

There are two kinds of software – system and application.

Operating systems and user interfaces

Examples of operating systems are the different versions of Windows, DOS, Linux and MacOS. An operating system is a complicated collection of pieces of system software which controls the operation of different computer resources. An operating system has to make the following things work.

- The filing system. It should let users load and save files onto disks, and do other things such as changing file names and creating folders.
- The memory. It must control the use of memory, so that different programs will run in different parts of memory and not interfere with each other.
- The input and output devices. The operating system uses device drivers to make sure input and output devices work properly.
- Programs. The operating system must enable the user to load application programs from disk into memory and have them run properly.
- The user interface. This is the way the user 'talks' to the computer, through the keyboard, mouse and screen. Through the user interface the user must input what they want to happen (e.g. running a program, saving, printing or deleting a file). Also through the user interface the operating system outputs results, such as a message confirming a file is being deleted.

JARGON DRAGON

A device driver is a small piece of software used to control something like a printer. Each different printer has its own device driver, supplied when the printer is purchased.

Character-based interfaces

Operating systems like DOS and UNIX use a character-based interface. This means the user types in commands through the keyboard, and the output appears usually without graphics. In the figure opposite the user (working in DOS) has

1 Used the date command to display the current date.
2 Used the cd (change directory)command to move to a new directory or folder – in this case, the directory called 'adobe'.
3 Used the dir command to list the files and folders.

```
E:\>date
The current date is: Thu 26/08/1999
Enter the new date: (dd-mm-yy)

E:\>cd adobe

E:\adobe>dir
  Volume in drive E has no label
  Volume Serial Number is 40C2-A987

  Directory of E:\adobe

06/04/98  11:36          <DIR>          .
06/04/98  11:36          <DIR>          ..
06/04/98  16:40          <DIR>          photoshop
            3 File(s)              0 bytes
                1,527,059,456 bytes free

E:\adobe>
```

GUIs

GUI stands for graphical user interface. Examples are Windows, MacOS, X Windows in UNIX and Gnome in Linux. A GUI usually has the following features:

- Windows – rectangular areas of the screen in which programs run. Windows can be moved, minimised, maximised, resized, closed, and can overlap each other. They are an efficient way of using the screen area.
- Icons – small pictures representing programs or options.
- A pointer on the screen which the user can control with a mouse on the desk.
- Buttons and other controls which the user operates using the mouse pointer.

Study Skills

Learning to use software

You will need to learn how to use many pieces of software. Here are some suggestions.

- *Look at the screen* – most software tells you what to do, if you look carefully and read the messages.
- Use on-screen Help.
- If in doubt, guess.
- If something goes wrong, try Edit Undo.
- Do not be afraid to try things out – you cannot do any harm.
- Spend a lot of time with the software.

The skills in this activity are essential for completing this unit's assignment. Find out how to do the following tasks on the computers you use, and practice them to make sure you can do them. The details will depend on what software you use and what you are allowed to do.

a The computer has a battery-powered clock with which it keeps track of the date and time. The operating system will let you adjust this. Change the system time and date.

b Change a security password setting. Check with your teacher. You might be able to change a CMOS password, or a user's logon password, or the password on a word processing or spreadsheet file.

c Use anti-virus software to virus-check some disks. If possible, set up the software so that it will automatically run a check every week.

d Change the appearance of the screen, such as by changing the colour of the title bars of windows, changing the 'wall-paper' or screensaver.

e Create some new folders.

**Remember –
User interfaces**

Either GUI or
character based

3.3 *Computer programming*

Computer programming means:

* creating software – producing it from 'scratch'
* testing it – making sure it always works and finding any 'bugs'
* developing software, producing new versions, removing bugs
* preparing software for the user, for example by writing manuals.

Programming a computer takes time, knowledge, skill and aptitude. Most people who use a computer do not do any programming – they have neither the ability nor the need. On the other hand, programming in one form or another gives you great control over what the computer will do.

Important points you should check when setting out to write a program:

* Do you know clearly what you are trying to achieve?
* Is there a program available which does the job already?
* What is the best software to use to write the program, and are you very familiar with it?
* Do you know how you will test the result, so you will know if you have been successful?

Computer programming can take many different forms. The techniques used in this unit are:

- creating templates
- creating macros
- designing and producing hypertext documents using HTML
- customising applications.

Major pieces of software, such as generic applications or operating systems, are not produced in this way. They are written by teams of programmers, coding programs using **general-purpose languages** such as C++. This is done using software called **compilers** and **interpreters**. An example that you may have seen is Visual Basic.

One simple form of programming is setting up **templates**. A template is a 'model' document which is the starting point for the documents the user produces. For example, a word-processing template would probably set the page size and orientation, the margins, headers and footers, page numbering, and graphics such as a company logo. A spreadsheet template would probably have column headings set up, cell colours, border and shading, and (most importantly) the formulae in place.

Using templates saves the user time in setting up all the required features for *every* document, and means they will not make mistakes in doing so. It also makes sure that there is a uniform 'style' to all the documents they produce.

Templates are usually easy to create. The document features needed are set up, then it is saved, selecting the file type as 'template', and saving it into a special folder. After that, when a new document is created, the new template can be selected for it.

Activity 6

Make sure you can create templates by checking with this very simple example. Set up a word-processing template, with A4 paper size and landscape orientation. Have a left-hand margin of 3 inches, and a footer showing the page number and the date. Save this template, then create a document based on it. Print out the document to check it.

3.4 Macro programs

Another form of programming is to use **macros**. A macro is a short piece of program code which works in an application such as a word processor or a spreadsheet. Usually a user sets up a macro if he or she has to do the same thing lots of times. A macro will do it for them. Macros could be used to do things such as:

- save the current file, print it, then close it
- insert a graphic such as a company logo
- select some cells in a spreadsheet and clear them
- copy a table cell to all the other cells
- convert all the files in a folder to another format
- convert to and from inches and centimetres, inserting text in document
- calculate number of days between the present and a future date
- delete current line
- repeat last find
- run Windows Calculator – or another program
- print odd- or even-numbered pages
- save a file and copy it to a floppy disk
- provide a quick word count.

Macros can be set up in different ways. They can be obtained by:

- Writing the coded instructions in the special macro programming language of the application. This method gives you great scope for what you can make the macro do, but you have to learn the language, and it is easy to make mistakes.

- Using a macro 'recorder'. This is something which records what the user does. The user starts the recorder running, then does what the macro is supposed to do, then stops the recorder. This is an extremely easy method.
- A combination of the last two – recording the macro, then editing the code it produces.
- Using macros supplied with the package, or obtaining others from 'macro libraries' on the Internet – but check for viruses.

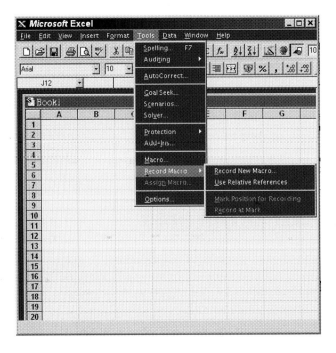

A macro being set up in Microsoft Excel

Macros are run by using a key combination (such as CTRL and 'a'), or by choosing from a menu, or a button in a toolbar (when the macro is created, it can be assigned to one of these). This makes it very easy for the user to run the macros.

> Many computer viruses are in the form of macros, so care must be taken. Some organisations remove macro options from applications because of the virus threat.

Activity 7

Produce a 'delete current line' macro in a word processor as follows:

- Start a new document and type in a few lines of text – it does not matter what you type. Put the cursor on one line.
- Start the macro recorder.
- Select the current line of text.
- Press 'Delete' to delete it.
- Stop the macro recorder.
- Assign the macro to a key combination, or better, to a new button on a toolbar.
- Check the macro works.

Remember – Macros

- Within applications
- Short pieces of program
- Used to automate common tasks

3.5 HTML programs

HTML stands for Hypertext Mark-up Language. Hypertext means that that there are links in the document from one part to another. HTML is the format for documents on the World Wide Web on the Internet. HTML documents are normally viewed with some software called a browser, such as Microsoft Internet Explorer or Netscape Navigator.

Links are usually pieces of text which are <u>underlined</u> and shown in a different colour. When the mouse cursor moves over a link, it changes from a pointer to a hand with a finger pointing, and the status bar at the bottom of the window tells you the Web address of where the link leads. Graphics can also be made into links. When you click on the link, the browser will try to load that Web page. After you have visited several sites, clicking the Back and Forward buttons on the browser will return you to the places you have just visited.

Activity 8

If you have not done so before, spend some time on the Internet. Make sure you are familiar with the idea of following links.

An HTML document is made of the actual text which you see in the browser, and extra information coding for the appearance of the text and links. This extra information is in the form of **tags**. HTML has a large set of different tags which can be used for different purposes. For example, suppose you want part of the text in a page to appear in bold:

```
This is in bold.
```

The actual HTML document would look like this:

```
This is in <B>bold</B>
```

This uses the pair of tags `<B>` and `</B>`. The `<B>` tells the browser to start displaying the text in bold, and the `</B>` tells it when to stop.

There are two ways to produce HTML documents. One is to use a text editor, such as Notepad in Windows, and simply type in the text of the document together with the tags – like `<B>` and `</B>`. The file is then saved with a .htm extension, which is the standard for HTML documents. If a browser like Internet Explorer is running, the document can be loaded into it as a local file and checked to see that it looks correct. To use this method you have to learn HTML coding.

quick fire

What does HTML stand for?

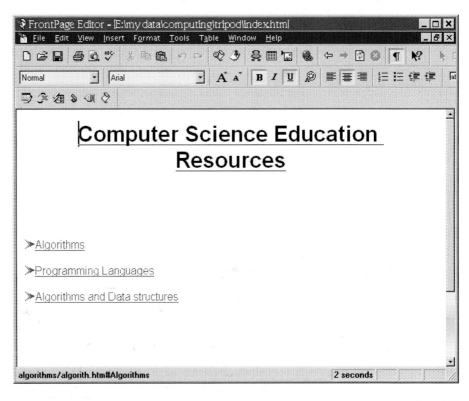

Creating an HTML page using Microsoft FrontPage

JARGON DRAGON

A *text editor* is a fairly simple program used to enter and edit text. It cannot handle any formatting such as bold or italic. It will usually save files only as 'pure text', containing nothing apart from what has been typed in.

The easier method is to use an *HTML editor.* These are software packages which let you produce web pages 'at the click of a button'. Examples are Microsoft FrontPage, Netscape Composer within the Communicator suite, and Adobe Pagemill. Editors like these provide the following facilities:

- changing the background colour or background image on a page
- formatting text in terms of size, font, colour, bold, italic, underline and so on
- working with tables
- inserting graphics
- working with links
- switching to a browser to check the appearance of the page.

These actions can be carried out very easily, by clicking buttons, rather than having to enter the HTML tags directly.

Graphics in HTML pages

A graphic in an HTML page is kept as a separate file, not 'embedded'. The HTML page contains a tag which tells the browser 'display a graphics file at this point'.

The graphics formats you can use are *gif* and *jpeg.* The browser itself can display these formats. If you use a different format, such as a Windows *bitmap* (.bmp), the browser will probably start Paintbrush and display it in that window, or even say that it does not know what to do with the file.

JARGON DRAGON

Even though all computer graphics are stored as binary patterns, there are many variations in exactly how this is done – and these are what *graphics formats* are. Each major graphics program has its own format, but most good programs can 'read' the other common formats.

Another reason for using gifs or jpegs is that these files are **compressed**, which means they are smaller (take up fewer bytes) than they would be otherwise. This is important so that they do not take a long time to download over the Internet. All the same, you should avoid using large pictures, because even when compressed they will still be slow to down load.

Browsers are also able to display animated gifs. You insert these into Web pages with an HTML editor the same as any graphic, but the browser will show you a moving picture.

There are three ways to obtain graphics for HTML.

1 It is easy to copy any picture from a Web page. On a PC, click with the right-hand mouse button on the picture, then choose 'Save as' and save it as a file on a disk. This applies to any type of graphic, including backgrounds, bullets, buttons, icons and lines. You *must* make sure you are not breaking copyright when you do this.

2 There are many collections of Web gifs available, on CD-ROM and on the Internet. Many of the Internet ones are free. These are usually divided into categories (backgrounds, animated gifs, dividing lines and so on). Use a search engine to find them. Again, you *must* check copyright.

3 Produce your own graphic. Scan in photographs. Use graphics software. All you have to do is to save them as gif or jpeg format.

Activity 9

Try out an HTML editor, and make sure you can make use of all the facilities just described by producing your own homepage.

Good Web page design

As well as being able to make Web pages, you must try to produce *good* pages. Here are my Top 10 points about Web design:

1 The content – what you write and the pictures you use – is most important. This is more important than the colour of the text or *anything* else. Choose content related to the *purpose* of the site and the intended *audience*.

2 Once you have got an idea of content, plan the structure on paper – what pages you will have and how they will be linked. You *can* put everything into one file, but it is better to split it into several small ones. If possible get everything onto the screen at once to avoid scrolling. This also makes your pages faster to load.

3 Choose colours and fonts that are easy to read quickly. This is about contrast. Dark blue is easy to see against a white background, but very hard to read on a black background. Do not use flashing text.

4 Give all your pages a uniform appearance – same text colour and background and similar bullets and lines and so on. Choose a design you like for the first page, and then copy it for other pages.

5 Do *not* underline text. It will be mistaken for a link.

6 Use small graphics – nothing more than 50 Kb in size. Users will not wait for large graphics to load.

7 Think about the meanings of graphics. Don't just insert all the pictures you like. Users will try to find the meaning of a graphic. Is it a link? What is it for? You will mislead them if it's just there because you like it.

8 Do not use animated graphics without good reason. They are very distracting and can take a long time to load.

9 Use tables to get the right layout for the page. Do not use frames. If you do not know how to, it's not a problem, because you should not use them.

10 Check copyright. Do not use graphics or sound or text unless you know you have the right to.

Here are somebody else's design notes, taken off the Internet. These notes are by Peter Aitken, and you can find them on the Internet at http://www.pgacon.com/web_page_tips.htm

---

Top 10 Do's of Web Page Design

If you want a web site that will scare visitors away, frustrate them, annoy them, and lose potential customers here are the top 10 things to do (needless to say this is really a list of don'ts!).

1 Ooo, this black background looks really cool! Particularly with the dark purple text displayed on it.

2 Hey, I like this music so everyone else will like it too. I'll play it on my web page.

3 This animated button looks great. I'll add a dozen more to my page.

4 Why should I check my links? My visitors won't mind if some of them don't work.

5 If I use 8 frames on my page people can view everything at once. They'll love it!

6 I can make sure people see this material by opening a couple of new browser windows. No one will mind.

7 My page is so awesome that people will not mind wading through a bunch of ads to see it.

8 I have 10 really great pictures of my pet armadillo and I'm going to put them all on my web page. So what if they are 100,000 bytes each?

9 My page isn't finished – in fact there is nothing there but the title. Even so I am going to broadcast my URL to all the newsgroups and search engines.

10 I are a good speler and I no grammer so I dont need to prufreed my page or run a spel chekker.

Activity 10

On the Internet, use a search engine such as Alta Vista to look for 'web page design tips'

Remember – Graphics in Web pages

- Compressed format – gif or jpeg
- Should be small
- Can be animated

3.6 Standard ways of working

When working on this unit, you need to work in an appropriate way, as covered in Unit 1. As a refresher, here are some points you need to look at to make sure you get the assignment done properly and in on time.

- Plan your work to produce what is required to given deadlines.
- Keep a log of IT problems you met and how you solved them.
- Evaluate your work and suggest how it might be improved.
- Proofread your products (on screen) to ensure accuracy and economic use of material.
- Keep back-up copies of files on another disk or in another location.
- Save your work regularly using different filenames.

Be careful about viruses, especially in connection with anything you download off the Internet.

Respect confidentiality and copyright – especially with anything you download off the Internet (like graphics).

When setting up the system for the user, watch out that:

- cables and connectors are electrically safe and people will not trip over them
- consumables like floppy disks and printer paper are replaced
- VDUs, keyboards and chairs are correctly set up to avoid RSI and similar problems.

JARGON DRAGON

Repetitive strain injury (*RSI*) is a kind of injury which comes about if the same movement is repeated for many hours every day. A common form of RSI is 'carpal tunnel syndrome', which is damage to the wrist caused by using the keyboard for too long.

Key Terms

After reading this unit you should be able to understand the following words and phrases. If you do not, go back through the unit and find out, or look them up in the Glossary.

application software	*CPU*
BIOS	*display driver*
bit	*general-purpose language*
bus	*gigabyte*
byte	*GUI*
compiler	*hardware*
compression	*HTML*

hypertext
impact printer
ink-jet printer
integrated circuit
interface card
interlaced display
interpreter
kilobyte
laser printer
macro
megabyte
memory
micro-processor
monochrome VDU
motherboard

operating system
pixel
PSU
RAM
refresh rate
resolution
ROM
software
system software
tags
templates
terabyte
VDU
video card
volatility

Test Yourself

1 Give four examples of pieces of hardware.
2 What is a GUI?
3 Name four input devices.
4 What is the difference between ROM and RAM?
5 Why are document templates used?
6 Give an example of something a spreadsheet macro might do.
7 Name three graphics formats.
8 How can you obtain graphics for use in Web pages?
9 How can a virus get into a computer?
10 Is a disk volatile?

Assignment for Unit Three

KatPhlaps is a cattery. When people go on holiday or are working away from home, they can have their cats looked after by KatPhlaps. They keep cats in good accommodation, well-fed and with expert vets checking out the cats.

KatPhlaps have never used computers before, but they want to start now, and your task is to get them set up.

They will need only one computer. They want to be able to produce A4 'labels' to go on the cat houses, showing a photograph of the cat and its details, so they can keep track of which cat is which. They will use a spreadsheet to work out the bills for customers when they come to collect their cats. They also want to set up an Internet Web site to publicise KatPhlaps. They do not want to spend more money on all of this than is necessary.

▶▶

Get the Grade!

Here are the criteria against which you will be assessed.

To obtain a pass you must ensure that you:

- describe clearly what KatPhlaps are looking for, and clearly describe the hardware and software you are proposing, including the installation of the printer
- produce printouts showing you have created the directories, checked the system time and date, swapped mouse buttons, and set the wall-paper and screen saver
- produce printouts showing you have set up the template and macro correctly
- produce printouts showing how you planned and set up the Web pages
- work safely, producing accurate work and keeping back-ups.

To obtain a merit you must also ensure that you:

- make sure your hardware and software descriptions are easy to read, accurate and detailed
- produce clear descriptions of the HTML pages, the template and the macro, with notes about their purpose and how they work
- use your skills with the operating system, spreadsheet, word processor and HTML software to configure them in ways which would meet KatPhlaps' needs
- prove you have carefully checked your work and corrected any errors
- plan your work so that you can complete the assignment within the deadline set
- work independently without a lot of help from your teacher.

To obtain a distinction you must also ensure that you:

- make sure the Web pages are attractive, easy to read and use, and make good use of text, sound and graphics
- produce detailed descriptions of the Web pages in technical terms
- make improvements to the template and spreadsheet macro described here, to make them more efficient and effective
- edit the code of the HTML or macro to improve it, producing 'before and after' print outs and notes of what you have done.

Your tasks

- If possible, find a local cattery like KatPhlaps, or a vets, and find out their requirements. Try to arrange a visit and an interview.
- Identify what hardware they need. This should include which processor they should have, what clock speed, how much RAM, what interface cards, what drives and what input and output devices they should get. You must tell them how much this will cost. You must do this in the form of a report, where you explain your choices.
- You also need to select a suitable operating system and applications software to meet their needs. Again you must cost this, and write a report.
- You must also write a short report describing how you would go about installing and configuring the printer you have selected.
- KatPhlaps plan to store the photos of the cats in a folder called catpics, and the bills in a folder called bills. You must create these for them. You must check that the computer time and date is correct.
- The user is left-handed and they want the mouse buttons reversed.
- The GUI 'wall-paper' and screen saver should be appropriate for the business. You must produce printed copy and screen dumps showing you have done this.
- The labels to put on the cat houses should look like the one shown below. Make a template for this in the word processor. Print out the template, and some examples of it in use.

A4 landscape paper

space for cat photo

Name: _____
Gender: _____
Owner: _____
Date in: _____
Date out: _____
Notes: _____
_____
_____

KatPhlaps

- The bill that they want to be able to produce should be like the one below. Set this up as a template in a spreadsheet, with suitable formulas. Print it out.

▶▶

KatPhlaps Cattery Customer Bill

Date

Customer Name

Customer Address

Cat Name	Date In	Date Out	Days Stayed	Cost	Extras	Notes	Total

Net Total	
VAT	
Gross Total	

- Create a macro, which will:
  - save the spreadsheet
  - print it out
  - close the spreadsheet
  - open a new spreadsheet using the bill template
  - assign the macro to a button on a toolbar or a menu.
- Produce print-outs showing this works.
- Design and produce some Web pages publicising KatPhlaps.

Key Skills — Opportunity

Communication, level 2	When you are finding out user needs and describing what they want, you can:
	• Contribute to a discussion about a straightforward subject (C2.1a).
	• Read and summarise information from two extended documents about a straightforward subject (C2.2). One of the documents should include at least one image.
	When you describe the setup:
	• Write two different types of documents about straightforward subjects (C2.3). One piece of writing should be an extended document and include at least one image.

Design project

What is covered in this unit

At the end of this unit you will be asked to provide a fully completed IT project. This will include:

- project proposal notes
- design plans for the project
- a completed and working project
- an evaluation of the project.

Materials you will need to complete this unit:

- hardware and software necessary for the completion of your chosen information technology project.

Introduction

In this unit you will choose to work on an IT activity in which you are interested.

- This must be a major piece of work, which you will agree with your tutor before you start it.
- You may build up and improve on work that you have already done in other units, or start a new activity.
- You may work individually or in a group, but if you work in a group the project must be chosen so that:
  - all members of the group can be marked on all stages of the project
  - other members of the group can complete their work even if one person leaves the group.

You will use the knowledge and skills that you acquired in the other units to design and create tools to help other IT users to be more effective in their work or to improve the quality of their work.

To succeed in this unit you will create a software product or set of products of your choice. They *must* work and do what you intended them to do. You will also need to describe the product and evaluate your work.

This unit helps you to:

- identify an IT project that you will enjoy
- define the purpose of the project
- plan how to carry out the project
- use software to produce the required facilities or product

- test and evaluate your work
- understand and develop good practice in your use of IT.

For your portfolio assignment you will need to produce:

- your project proposal notes
- your design plans for the project
- the *finished*, *working* project
- an evaluation of your product.

In this unit you choose your own assignment with the agreement of your tutor. You will be assessed on how well you carry out this assignment and awarded a grade. This grade will be your grade for the unit.

Remember
Your project must work

4.1 Identifying a suitable project

Many people who use computers don't know what the computer can do. They can describe what they want to achieve, but they can't make the computer work as they want.

'Now, how do I get it to make a cup of tea?'

Case Study

Jan uses a spreadsheet

Jan had been using a computer for some time for producing letters and reports for her department. One day Colin asked her to produce some sales figures. He gave her all the figures and told her: 'Use a spreadsheet. Then if we have to alter a figure it will alter all the others automatically.' Colin never himself used a computer, but wished to sound knowledgeable. ▶▶

Jan did not want to admit that she had never used a spreadsheet and worked out how to use it without asking for help. She managed to produce this report:

		SALES FIGURES		JAN–MAR			STAR
		Unit Price:		Unit Price			SALES
	Widgets	£291.21	Wodgets	£312.83			
	Nos.	Value	Nos.	Value	Total Value	
Colin	578	£168,319.38	401	£125,444.83	£293,764.21	*
Pat	415	£120,852.15	521	£162,984.43	£283,836.58	
Zena	466	£135,703.86	483	£151,096.89	£289,800.75	
Total	1459	£424,875.39	1405	£439,526.15	£864,401.54	

Jan had used the spreadsheet only to format the data she had been given. She had entered all the numbers as numbers and had not used any formulae.

She was pleased with how it looked, and so was Colin but just before the meeting where Colin needed to produce the figures, he asked her to alter the unit cost of Widgets to £219.21 and print out five copies. Jan did this. Colin came back from the meeting in a very bad mood.

1 Why was Colin in a bad mood? What was wrong with the sales figures, and why? You may need to do some calculations.

2 If Jan had come to you for help before using the spreadsheet package, how could you have helped her?

3 After you help Jan with her spreadsheet, she tells you about another problem. She word-processes all the letters for her department, while three assistant managers in the department, Colin, Zena and Pat plan the letters. Each assistant manager has different ideas about how the letters should look, wanting different fonts, font sizes and margin sizes. They also have different standard paragraphs that they like to use. As Jan types the different letters, she spends a lot of time changing from one standard to another. How could you help her with this?

You can probably think of examples of computer facilities you have discovered during this course which have allowed you to use computers more efficiently than before. You should have learnt how to use a computer package to the full, and that it is worth studying a new computer package before using it.

Most computer users when given new software don't stop and learn to use the new facilities, but try to use it in the same way that they used the old software. This may well be true for computer users in your educational establishment, in a local business with which you are connected, a leisure club you belong to or computer users that are your friends or relatives.

For this unit you will need to identify a project that will help someone to make better use of their hardware and software. The project should ideally be a *real project* which provides something useful for a *real client*. Even if you do not have a real client, the project should be useful for computer users other than yourself.

Activity 1

a List possible clients for a computer project. These might be:
- people that you know who use a computer at home or for their work
- people you know who have a computer at home (perhaps someone else uses it) but do not use it at present
- people you know who are buying a computer, but have not had one before

- local businesses
  - that you work for part time
  - where you have had work experience
  - where you are a good customer
  - run by friends or relatives
  - that you know very well for other reasons
- clubs you belong to
- computer users within your school or college.

b What do these people use computers for now? What might they use a computer for in future? Do they have a hobby that they might use it for? You might need to interview them.

c Will they be prepared to give some time to you for the eventual project? Warn them that you will need to:
- interview them for information for your project before you start including asking them for test data
- check your design with them
- check the product with them at the end.

The project can be a single information technology product or a set of information technology utilities.

Example projects

Single products

- Standard design and layout templates for a magazine or newsletter. This should include lots of graphics and advertisements and you will need macros to set layouts and insert items. This might be useful for a club, a local business or your school or college or could be for a magazine you wish to produce.

Activity 2

St Ivel Swimming Club produces a programme for its swimming galas. It is eight pages long. Its cover page (page 1) has the same design each time with the club name and logo, a picture of the pool in use and the date and time of the gala together with the names of teams swimming in it. Page 2 contains an advertisement for the local sports shop that sponsors the programme. Page 3 lists the events in this gala. Pages 4 and 5 give club news including results of the last gala. Page 6 lists forthcoming events. Page 7 gives details of the club and how to join, and the back cover (page 8) has information about the swimming pool hosting the event. The programme has been set up as a template in a desktop publishing package, making it easy to bring out for each issue.

You could create such a template.

- A database of work contacts, fellow club members, friends and relations. There should be facilities to merge names and addresses into letters. This would be useful for any organisation or person who writes letters.

Activity 3

Connington Hall and Leisure Centre runs shows, concerts (classical, jazz, pop etc), films, dances, club nights and sports fixtures (badminton, table tennis, five-a-side football, roller blading). When customers buy tickets to an event, the centre enters their details on a database, together with their interests, and sends them information about future events that they might be interested in. They do not want to send everyone information about all events as this will give too high a postage bill. They also feel that individualised letters would be more friendly and attract the right customers.

You could design a database and mail merge system for a similar centre.

- A Web site with multiple pages. There should be good cross-referencing and facilities to keep it up to date. You could publicise a local business or manufacturer, a local club or even facilities at your educational establishment.

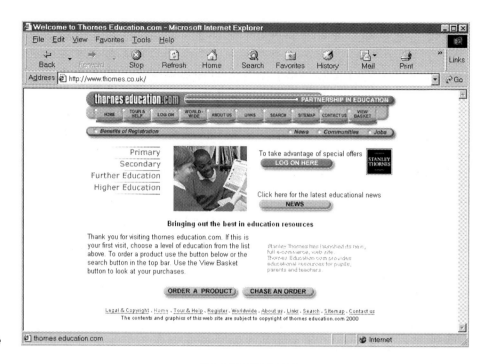

An example of a Web site

Activity 4

Connington Hall and Leisure Centre decides to set up a Web site to advertise over the Internet. They have an index which allows users to look for events by type and by date, after which the page with the appropriate information comes up.

From each type of entertainment page other types can be accessed and other local centres with similar types of entertainment can be accessed where the centres have agreed to advertise each others' entertainments and it is easy to return to the index page. From the date position, other dates can be scrolled up or down, other Web sites can be accessed if relevant and it is easy to return to the index page.

You could create a similar site.

- A system to keep club membership records up to date, including pictures of the members, payment details and records of their club activities. This could be useful for sports clubs, dramatic societies and other organisations.

Activity 5

St Ivel Swimming Club has a database for its members. Each member has a photo on the database so that it can be accessed easily if needed for the club news in the gala programme. Information is also kept as to which types of events they like to enter (swimming strokes, race lengths, types of dives), their age as they might want to enter events for children or oldies, records of previous events entered and their results.

Event organisers can then print out lists of members who might like to enter for the competitions organised. The members can be contacted individually and information is at hand which could be used in a club programme or newsletter.

A record of payment for club membership is also kept.

You might like to create a similar database.

- What software is available to you at school or college, or even at home, that you can use? There may be software to help you
  - create games
  - provide a variety of graphics, perhaps for printing on T-shirts, coasters, cards, labels
  - edit photos
  - learn languages
  - create music.
- Did you get interested in the work in a previous assignment? Would you like to expand upon work done in another unit?

Your product must be usable by someone else as well as you and must therefore be *foolproof*. Someone else using the product will not know what you had in mind when you built it. If, for instance, the user has to choose between doing two things there must be a message to explain this. The product should not hang if the user makes an error, and the user should be able to correct the error.

Utilities

You might prefer to work on a project that provides a number of more simple facilities for novice IT users. Some examples are given below.

- Set up easy ways for the user to access software that they use often. This could involve setting up menus, icons or program groups.
- Create file and folder structures to let the user store and retrieve work easily. You will need to find out how the user works and the different types of work required. If several users are sharing data or sharing a work space on the computer, you might need to include security measures so each user can keep their work safe.
- Set toolbars in software to allow the user to access facilities that they require easily. You will need to find out exactly the user's needs.
- Create macros in software to help the user work more efficiently. Examples might be checking data inputs, automatic formatting of reports, automatic calculations.
- Create templates to help the user work more efficiently. This could include page layout, paragraph styles, fonts, borders and shading.

- Set software options to suit the needs of the user. Set up suitable default options in a package.
- Create files of commonly used text or graphics to use as required. This is useful if someone writes standard types of letters. Some software has an autocorrect facility, which allows text or a graphic to automatically replace certain keystrokes.
- Create icons or files to let a user access an information service quickly. You might personalise an Internet user's home page.
- Write simple instructions on how to use a product.
- Use a scheduler, journal or calendar to take actions or prompt the user at a given time or date.
- Create a spreadsheet to meet a user's needs.
- Create a database to meet the user's needs.

This unit involves choosing, completing and documenting the project. It is important to choose your project carefully, so take your time.

Your time should divide up roughly thus:

- 25% to choose the right project, write the proposal and have it accepted
- 50% to create and test the work
- 25% to document and evaluate the work.

Look back over the work that you have completed in other units to see how long it took you.

Choose a project that is worth doing and that you will enjoy – but choose a project that you can finish *on time*.

Activity 6

a List the types of project that you think you would be able to carry out successfully on your own.

b List the types of project that you think you would be able to carry out successfully if working in a group. A group project would have to be bigger than an individual project.
- What strengths would you provide in the group?
- What strengths would you require from the other group members?

c Work in a group. Look at all the individual projects listed by the group members. For each project, decide
- What kind of IT design work is needed for the project?
- What resources are needed? The resources include application or operating system software, data files, clip art, CD-ROMs, input or output hardware, instruction manuals, textbooks, consumable materials such as paper, disks, ink, toner, people (and the time they will use) to tell you what they require, access to the Internet.

▶▶

- Each one of you in the group should end up with at least one, and preferably two or three, project ideas that you feel you could develop, and for which you have the resources. It is no good choosing a project which you cannot resource.

d Still in the group, look at all the group projects in turn.
- What kind of IT design work is needed for the project?
- How many people are needed for the project?
- How could you split up such a project so that each group member can work independently even if other members do not finish their part of the project?
- What resources are needed?
- Each group member should end up with a group project to which they would be happy to contribute.

e Working individually, identify two or three possible projects, or parts of bigger projects, that interest you and that you believe you can complete on your own. For each one note down your ideas for how you could develop the project or part of project:
- Who will be your main client?
- How will you get all the information you need for the project?
- How will you design the project?
- What resources will you use?
- How will you test your work?
- How long do you think the project will take?
- For a group project, who are the other group members?

4.2 Producing a project proposal

Example – working as a consultant

GNVQ Partners are a consultancy firm run as a partnership of several IT consultants. The firm is run by a number of directors who deal with the organisation of the company: dealing with administration, finance and providing hardware and software.

It is the job of the partners to:

- find customers
- sell them a consultancy project
- provide the consultancy
- evaluate the finished consultancy.

When you do your project you become a partner in GNVQ Partners and your teachers and lecturers are the directors.

Before you start a project you will need to get it approved by your directors (teachers). To get their approval you must produce a project proposal. A project proposal comprises brief but clear notes describing the project you will carry out and the expected result.

For your project proposal you will need

1 Title page to include:
   a Title of project
   Name of customer (if you do not have a real customer you will need to invent one)
   b Description of customer – if it is a business or other organisation what it does; if a person, their occupation
   c Your name/s.

> ## Spreadsheet to check value of shares
>
> for
> ## Mr Davey
> (retired)
>
>
> by
> ## Chris Jellings

2 Description of user needs. This should be about half to one page of A4 and include:

  a what they want done

  b how they do it now

  c what improvements they expect.

3 Meeting the needs: how you intend to meet these needs (half to one page of A4)

  a what software you will use

  b what you will do with the software – e.g. customise it, create templates, create macros, set up a database.

---

3 a Spreadsheet
  b Make outline spreadsheet where Mr. Davey can enter his shares and what they are worth every Saturday.

    Make graphs to show him how his investments are going up and down.

4 a, b Mr Davey has a computer running Excel so I can make the spreadsheet at college.

  c I will need a disc to transfer it to his machine.

  d I will need to check Mr Davey's version of Excel. I will need to find out from Mr Davey more about shares and how he knows the value of the shares. I may need the Help on Excel.

---

4 List of resources required

  a hardware

  b software

  c media

  d research materials.

5 Expected results. Depending on your project, this could be a sketch, a list, a description, or may have been covered in section 2.

---

5 Graph showing how his shares are doing

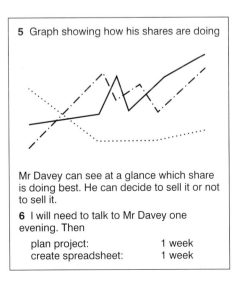

Mr Davey can see at a glance which share is doing best. He can decide to sell it or not to sell it.

6 I will need to talk to Mr Davey one evening. Then

| plan project: | 1 week |
| create spreadsheet: | 1 week |

155

6 Time schedule. Once you have approval you will need to:

  a plan the project in detail

  b create and test the product or facilities (this may involve several stages – if so, list the stages)

  c document it.

Estimate the length of time needed for each item in the project, bearing in mind anything else that you might be doing at the same time. Make allowances for things to go wrong. Write out a realistic schedule for the work – i.e. for each item give rough start and finish dates. In a real consultancy the estimated time will be used to calculate the price of the project.

7 If you have a real customer – check the proposal with them to see that you have understood their needs correctly.

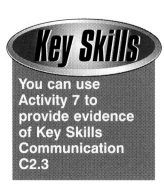

You can use Activity 7 to provide evidence of Key Skills Communication C2.3

Activity 7

a What goes on the title page of your project proposal?

b What are the three areas covered for user needs?

c Name three possible media that might be listed under resources.

d Name two pieces of information which will help you estimate how long the project will take you to produce.

e Write up your project proposal using standard ways of working.

4.3 Getting permission to go ahead

You will need to present your proposal notes to your directors to get approval to go ahead.

You will be asked questions about your proposal, so you may need to argue the case for it Make sure that you know *exactly* what you want to do before making your presentation.

You will need to convince your directors that your project is worthwhile and you must show that you can complete it in time without help using available resources.

Prepare yourself for the meeting with the directors

Your course assessor will be at the meeting where you present your case to the directors. You will present your case verbally, covering:

* the purpose of the project
* the user requirements

Make sure you look smart for the presentation

- the resources required
- the proposed time scale.

You will be questioned on your presentation and will hand in your written proposals at the end of it.

Prepare for the presentation by practising it with a friend.

- Your friend should make sure that your proposal makes sense.
- They should understand exactly what you intend doing and should tell you if they don't.
- They should point out any problems in your proposal and ask questions about how you will achieve the end result.
- The more critical they are, the better the friend they are.

Make any necessary corrections.

- Take particular trouble over your timing.
- Look back at similar work that you have done before. How long did it take you? Be realistic. It will take you just as long next time.
- How much help did you have? You will need to do it this time without help. Can you convince your directors that you can finish on time?

You MUST FINISH your project on time

Stick this notice on your mirror!

If you are working in a group, you can act as friends for each other. In your time schedule, make sure you have regular meetings planned to check how you are all getting on.

| Activity 8 |

a What are the four key topics in your presentation to your assessor?

b Make the presentation to your assessor. Keep a copy, which should have been signed by your assessor.

4.4 Planning the design

It is often helpful to work in a project team, where you can help each other with ideas. You will have to do this, of course, if you are working on a group project.

If you are working on individual projects, try working with others during the planning stage. It is much harder to plan the project than to start producing it. Describing your plan to your team-mates should help.

JARGON DRAGON

A *project team* is a group of people working together on a project.

Make arrangements for the group to meet often to discuss how you are getting on. Meetings should be short and fairly frequent. You might like to try meeting for 20 minutes every morning to start off your working day, or you might find 10 minutes three times a day suits you better. Find the best way of working for your group for this stage of the project.

Running a planning meeting

Start your meetings on time. Do not wait for late-comers. Keep minutes of the meeting and stick to the agenda.

The *minutes* should include:

1 Start time of meeting.
2 People present and apologies from people absent. If people come late, their time of arrival should be recorded.
3 Reports on the agenda items.

Minutes of meeting 3/3/99 9.00am

Present Mo, Jo, Ali – 9.10

Away Chris

Jo tried to ring Chris last night but got no reply. Will try going round tonight.

1. Mo's Mum has agreed to provide information for making a database about the knitted dolls that she makes and sells. This will take about 1 hour.

   Jo will get information from the secretary of the cycle club about future events for their website. Has made a list of local bike shops and will ask them if they want to sponsor the site. Ali and Jo will go round together.

   Ali has spoken to Jan who is pleased to be given help. She has explained what she wants. Ali will sort out her problems with the word-processing.

2. Mo will do screen, print, report and record layouts for tomorrow.

   Jo will do screen layouts and mark cross references to other web pages within the cycle club web pages and with other web pages of interest.

   Ali to design icons and find out how to create own icons. Also design toolbars for Jan.

Next meeting – 1.45 today – agenda item – will we be able to get it done by tomorrow, or will we need help.

Meeting closed at 9.30.

The *agenda* should include:

1 Matters arising from last minutes. This should include checks against the minutes of the last meeting that people have completed the tasks set.
   a If they have completed their tasks, they should demonstrate what they have done to the group, and the rest of the group will check that they understand what has been done
   b If they have not completed the tasks, they should explain the problem, and the rest of the group can help them to sort it out.
2 Tasks to be carried out before the next meeting. These tasks should be

a short enough to be completed by the next meeting (this will mean that long tasks should be split up into smaller parts)

b long enough that no one wastes time – plan ahead.

3 Time check, i.e. check that the planning stage will be finished on time.

4 Date, time and agenda for next meeting.

What is included in the planning

The design of each project will be different. Here is a list of the sort of design plans you might need, although you will need to produce your own list of design plans to match the task in your project. Sketch out in note form or as a diagram or drawing.

1 The information you need:

   a Does your project need real data – e.g. for a Web site or database?

   b Does it need test data – e.g. for a magazine layout or a spreadsheet?

   c What general information do you need for your project – e.g. for customising software for a user?

   d What are the sources for the information you need?

Jo's Plan

1. Mum is helping and will give me half hour every evening after I help with washing up.

2. Create database and create records.
(see layout), create entry screens.
Enter five customers and five dolls and five orders.
Make test data and test entry screens.
Make notes of what I do for technical documentation.
Make notes for user documentation and check with Mum.   10 hours

3. Create reports (see layouts)
Design test data and use it for testing reports.
Make notes of what I do for technical documentation.
Make notes for user documentation and check with Mum.   10 hours

4. Enter rest of data for Mum   2 hours

5. Test system   2 hours

6. Check with Mum $\frac{1}{2}$ hour

7. Make alterations that she wants   5 hours?

8. Write up technical documentation   2 hours

9. Write up user documentation and check with Mum.   2 hours

10. GIVE IN!!!

---

2 Who can help you with the planning:

   a the project customer?

   b friends acting as customers?

   c tutors and colleagues?

3 Example layouts – you will need diagrams for all:

   a screen layouts

   b print layouts

   c report layouts

   d templates

   e record layouts

   f complex data types.

Screen Layout   Ali

Icon for Zena

JARGON DRAGON

The *layout* is the detailed design of a screen, document or data type showing exactly where text and images and fields will be placed on screen or on paper, and showing the exact lengths and types of data.

4 Descriptions of purpose for any:
   a computer program
   b macro
   c formula.

5 Lists of:
   a graphic images – plus sketches of each
   b sounds – plus descriptions of each
   c other objects – plus descriptions of each
   d connections to other parts of the project.

6 Examples of:
   a records
   b data types
   c calculations
   d formulae used.

7 Specifications for:
   a sort requirements
   b search requirements
   c checking user inputs
   d menus
   e toolbars
   f icons.

```
Specs for Jan            Ali

Icons for Colin's work
           Zena's work
           Pat's work

Each icon will take Jan to Word in the
appropriate working directory.

She will choose the template from the
template menu.

Standard paragraphs will be in
appropriate directory.
```

8 Name and describe:
   a software tools to be used
   b other facilities used.

9 Test plan to include:
   a ideas to test each part of the project – plus test data. You may even
      want to test the design before continuing with the project (see below)
   b ideas to test completed project – plus test data.

161

10 Production plan to include:
   a list of tasks to be performed to complete the project
   b each task:
      i to be linked to its data, specifications tests etc. as described in 1–7 above
      ii to have notes made for technical documentation
      iii to have notes made for the user documentation
      iv to be given a target time for completion.

Testing the design

If you have a real customer, take the design back to them for checking that the project will produce what they require.

If you do not have a real customer, go through it with your project team, who should act as customers.

/ **Activity 9** /

a Plan your design.
b Produce the plans.
c Keep copies of minutes of project team meetings.
d Follow standard ways of working.

4.5 Production and progress monitoring

You should by now have a list of tasks needed to create your project. For each task you should have the time that you think it should take. For example:

- Set up the Word template called 'Colin' for Jan with 5 cm margins and his name in Script font as a footer. Normal font will be Times New Roman size 16. 1.5 spacing.   3 hours
- Find out how to create a macro to open a new template as Colin automatically. Try manual? Try big Word book in library. Ask the technician?   5 hours?
- Create a macro to open a new template as Colin automatically.   1 hour
- Do same for Zena and Pat.   ½ hour
- Make notes for technical documentation.   1 hour
- Check which toolbars Jan wants.   ½ hour
- Find out how to create my own icons. Ask Lou, who probably has a program to do this.   3 hours
- Create icons.   3 hours
- Check the work completed with Jan.   ½ hour
- Write out user documentation.   3 hours

- Check it, with spelling and grammar checkers.   ½ hour
- Check it by eye for consistency of style.   ½ hour

When you start to create your project you must check the time that you take for a task against the time that you set yourself. If you do not do this carefully, you may find that you take ages over one small piece of the project and run out of time for the rest.

> ## Keep the Project
> ## Moving Forwards

It is important that you finish the project. If you have time left over when you have finished, then go back and improve on tasks that you are not yet happy with.

If you keep your working group from your planning stage, the other group members should be able to help you to keep the project moving.

Activity 10

a Produce your project.
b Keep any documents produced at this stage in your portfolio.
c Keep back-up copies of work produced.
d Keep copies of project team minutes.
e Follow standard ways of working.

4.6 Testing and documentation

The test plan

You will need to test:

- all user inputs to allow for user errors
- all outputs to show they work as planned
- all calculations, formulae and macros to see they work correctly
- separate parts of a project
- the whole project together.

The test plan should include:

- test data to be used
- expected outcome of test with the test data.

When you produce your test plan you should think what should happen if:

What sort of errors could a user make when inputting?

- users press the wrong keys (they should be able to correct their errors; they should get a helpful message to tell the user what key or keys are required)
- users enter incorrect information (they should be able to correct their errors)
- several keys are pressed together, in particular if a shift or control key is one of the keys pressed
- macros are used incorrectly
- exceptional values of data are entered – e.g. out of range values, wrong types of values, values input to end data entry
- information is entered in the wrong place – e.g. the user puts an end-date in a start-date field and vice versa.

You also need to test that:

- all the facilities you provided work as you meant them to
- reports produced by your product meet the user's needs
- documents produced meet the user's needs
- calculations give correct results.

When writing your test plan, you should list the results you expect for your test data, and when you do the tests you should be able to tick off all the results as correct.

The way to test a product is to try to stop it working properly. You may find it helpful to get a friend who is unfamiliar with your project to test your product too. They are more likely to do the unexpected than you are. If they find a fault then you must work out a way of handling the situation so that it doesn't happen again.

What should you try to do when testing your project?

Remember
A good test crashes the program!

Record all tests as you make them. You should tick each test on the test plan if the outcome is correct. If not, note the actual outcome and explain what you did to overcome the problem.

Activity 11

a Test your product.
b Keep notes of all your testing.
c Follow standard ways of working.

Documentation

There are two types of documentation.

Technical documentation should be written while creating a product as it acts as a reminder to you as you go along. At this stage you should just need to tidy up your notes and sort them into an order.

Technical documentation consists of notes made to show how you created the project. These are useful if you want to alter the way it works at a later stage or do something similar again.

The documentation is for a technician working on the project, not for the user of the software.

All technical documentation should include:

- the name of task completed (if you are working for a large organisation it may also have a code number)
- a brief description of the task completed
- the date it was completed, or altered
- the name of the person completing (or altering) the task
- notes on how the task was completed, so that someone reading your notes will be able to do something similar.

User documentation is for the user to understand how to use the product. It should include:

- the name of the product
- what the product does
- how to use it
- how to get out of trouble if you use it wrongly.

It should be given to the user together with the product.

What are the two types of documentation?

User documentation contains an explanation to a user of how to use a product. It could take the form of a user manual, notes on how to use facilities, on-line help.

Activity 12

a Document your work.
b If you have a real user, deliver the product and documentation and ask them for their opinion.
c Follow standard ways of working.

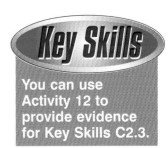

You can use Activity 12 to provide evidence for Key Skills C2.3.

4.7 Evaluation

A review of your work is essential.

- Did you manage the design and creation tasks well?
- What worked well and what worked less well in your project?
- How would you improve the product if you were given more time and better resources?
- Can you easily use your design on other computers?
- Have you used techniques that you might use again?
- What do users think of your product?

Writing an evaluation helps you to understand what you have learnt in completing the project and can make your next project easier to design.

You must learn to be systematic in your evaluation.

1 Did you meet the time schedule for the design and creation activities?
2 How well does the finished product meet its design specification?
3 What advantages does your product offer the user in terms of:
   a ease of use
   b speed of use
   c quality
   d any others?
4 What are the disadvantages of the product in terms of:
   a time
   b cost
   c failures
   d poor specification
   e any others?

Activity 13

a Evaluate your project.
b Use standard ways of working.
c Keep the evaluation in your portfolio.

4.8 Standard ways of working

These are described in detail in Unit 1. The following is a shortened version of these requirements written to apply specifically to this unit.

To develop good practice in your use of IT you must:

- proofread your work to ensure accuracy
- keep back-up copies of files on another disk and in another location
- save work regularly using different filenames
- keep information free from viruses
- respect confidentiality
- respect copyright.

/ **Activity 14** /

a Check through your portfolio to make sure that you have worked according to the standard ways of working.

b Make sure you have all the evidence that you need in your portfolio.

Assignment for Unit Four

You need to produce:

- project proposal notes
- design plans for the product
- a completed and operational product (or products)
- an evaluation of your work.

Get the Grade!

Here are the criteria against which you will be assessed.

To obtain a pass you must ensure that you:

- describe clearly the purpose of the project, the user requirements, the resources required and the proposed timescale
- produce clear design plans that specify the timescale, what is to be produced and accurate details of each of the component parts such as screen layouts, storage structures and processing requirements
- create a working product or set of products that is appropriate for user needs and operates according to the design plans
- show clearly what tests you used to check the operation of your product to ensure that it was complete, accurate and operational
- show you can work safely when setting up equipment, check the accuracy of your work and keep backup copies of all files.

To achieve a merit you must also ensure that you:

- create a substantial product that includes the selection, configuration and effective use of software to meet an identified need
- produce accurate, attractive and easy-to-read descriptions and design plans with clearly stated objectives and detailed definitions of all component parts of the project, including clearly annotated copy of any screen dumps or printed output

- show you have checked your work and corrected obvious errors
- organise the presentation of your work so that it shows clearly how you progressed from ideas and design to completion of the project
- show you can work independently to produce the product and that you monitored progress against your plan to ensure it was completed within the agreed timescale.

To achieve a distinction you must also ensure that you:

- show a broad understanding of IT systems in an evaluation of your work, including well written commentary on the views of users, the quality of the product, ways in which it could be improved and possible alternative methods of achieving similar results
- show imaginative design ideas in your product and demonstrate that it measurably improves user efficiency and/or output quality
- show you can adapt your work plan appropriately to overcome any problems experienced during production.

Key Skills   Opportunity

Communications	You have opportunities in this unit to demonstrate all Communications Key Skills.

Glossary

Use this glossary as a quick way of checking the meanings of words. In the explanations, words in italics can also be found in the glossary. For fuller explanations, see the main text.

absolute reference
In a spreadsheet, a *cell reference* that does not change when the *formula* is copied or moved to another cell. It refers to a fixed location

account statement
A *document* sent by one company to a customer, which lists all the transactions within a month or a quarter, and gives the total owed

agenda
A *document* which lists the points to be dealt with in a meeting

application software
A *software* package which uses the computer to solve a real-world problem. Not *system software*

back-up
A copy of files made for safe keeping in case there is some problem with the computer

BIOS
Basic Input Output System – *system software* which carries out basic control of input and output devices

bit
A binary digit – a zero or a one. All digital *data* is coded as bit patterns

bookmark
In a Web *browser*, sites can be bookmarked. This means they are added to a list of favourite places, making it easy to return to them later on

Boolean
A data type which is either true or false. See *logical data type*

browser
A piece of *software* used to view *Web pages* on the Internet

bullet points
Small circles, squares or other symbols used to highlight items in a list

bus
A set of wires which carry data around inside a computer at very high speed

business card
> A small card carrying someone's name and contact details, given to someone so they can get in touch again

business letter
> A formal letter about business matters

byte
> A unit of data, made of 8 *bits*

cell reference
> In a spreadsheet formula, a way of referring to a cell. For example B3 means the contents of the cell at column B row 3

clip art
> A collection of graphic images. From this a picture can be selected to be used in a document

compiler
> A piece of *system software* which translates a program into codes the computer can recognise

compression
> Coding data so it takes up fewer *bytes*. Internet data and files on disk are often compressed

confidentiality
> Making sure *information* is restricted to people who have a right to see it. Personal data is usually private and confidential

configuration
> The details of how a system is arranged, organised and set up

copyright
> The legal right of someone who creates something to control its use. Graphics, music, writing and programs all belong to whoever produced it

country settings
> Part of the *configuration* of a computer which makes it suitable for use in a certain country – such as the currency and time zone settings

CPU
> Central processing unit – the part of the computer which can run programs

currency data type
> A *data type* concerned with amounts of money

data
> Basic items of knowledge like numbers, letters, dates, *pixels* and so on. See *information*

data type
> What kind of thing the data item is – like numbers or text and so on

database

A database is a structured store of *data*, usually on a computer system.

default

A default value or setting is the value obtained unless the user changes it. What you get if you don't change it

desktop publishing

Producing text and pictures in columns and boxes well formatted as in a newspaper or magazine, on a small computer

display driver

A piece of *system software* which controls a *video card* and *VDU*

document

On a computer, a piece of work someone produces, such as a word-processed text or a spreadsheet or a graphic image. Documents can be stored on disk. They can also be on paper, printed out or written by hand

documentation

Software documentation is a set of documents about a package or a project. User documentation is the same as a user manual. Technical documentation records how something works, and is intended for the use of programmers

electronic format

Documents stored in a way that computers can use, such as on disk or sent by *email*. The alternative is to have them on paper.

e-mail

Documents sent from a user on one computer, stored temporarily on a server, then picked up by the other person on their computer

ethical

Something is ethical if it is the right thing to do. The same as moral

exception

An unusual or incorrect item of data

fax (header)

This is a picture of a document sent between fax machines or computers over a telephone line. A fax header is the first page, and it gives details like who the fax is from and to, how many pages long it is, and the date and time it was sent. Fax is short for facsimile

field

In a database table, one of the columns

filename

Documents and programs are stored in a computer system in files. Each file has a different filename, which should be chosen to reflect what the file is about.

flyer

A flyer is a document, often a single page, used to advertise a product or event. A flyer is given out by hand or by post

folders

A folder is a way of organising the storage of files. A folder can be set up to contain a set of related files. Folders can also contain other folders. Sometimes called directories.

font

A design for the shapes of the letters of the alphabet

foreign key

A *field* in a *table* which is the *primary key* in another table

formula

In a spreadsheet a formula is placed in a cell so a calculation will be done. It usually contains *cell references*. An example is A1+B2

function

Used in spreadsheet formulas and programming, a function is something which works out a value. Example functions are average and square root

general-purpose language

A programming language which can be used to write a wide range of types of programs. Examples are Basic and Pascal

gigabyte

One thousand million *bytes*

grammar checker

This is a common *tool* in a word processor. It checks that the text is free from grammatical errors, unlike what this sentence is

GUI

Graphical user interface. Using graphics on the screen to make the system user friendly. Most GUIs use windows, *icons* and a mouse

hardware

The actual machinery of the computer, in contrast to *software*

header and footer

A header is a piece of text which appears at the top of the page, in the top margin. A footer appears in the bottom margin. A page number is often placed in the footer

HTML

Hypertext mark-up language. The way the layout of Web pages is coded

hypertext

This has links between and within documents

icon

A small picture, usually representing a program in a *GUI*

impact printer

A printer that works by hammering letter-shapes onto paper through an inked ribbon

indent

Setting the edge of some text further in from the left or right than normal

index

In a book, an index is a list of all the items in the book, in alphabetical order, together with their page number. A file index is a similar idea – it makes it faster to find data in the file

information

Meaningful facts. Pieces of *data* in a certain context with meaning makes information

ink- jet printer

A printer which works by squirting tiny droplets of ink onto paper

integer

A whole number

integrated circuit

A very small electronic circuit inside a 'chip' case. An integrated circuit may contain millions of components

interface card

A card carrying integrated circuits which is used to connect between a *motherboard* and a peripheral device like a printer

interlaced display

A type of *VDU* display where the adjacent rows of dots are displayed alternatively

interpreter

A piece of *system software* which can run another program. A Basic program is usually run by an interpreter

invoice

A document sent by a business to a customer after they have sent the customer some goods. The invoice details the goods and how much the customer is being charged for them

itinerary

An itinerary plans a journey, listing where people are going, when they are travelling, where they will stay and so on

justification

Which side of the page text is lined up at. Text is either left justified, right justified or centred

key (primary, secondary, foreign)

A key is a *field* in a *table* used to search for data. A primary key has unique values which identify each row. A secondary key is a field other than the primary key used to locate data. A *foreign key* is a primary key in another table

kilobyte

One thousand *bytes*

laser printer

A printer which works by a laser beam and an electrostatic drum

layout grid

A rectangular array of dots marking locations. This makes it easier to line up text and graphics neatly in a document. Software often has a 'Snap to grid' option to make this quicker

line spacing

How far apart the lines of text are

log

A record of events, with times and dates and details. For example an error log is a record of what has gone wrong

logical data type

A *data type* which is either true or false – sometimes called a *Boolean* value

logo

A logo is a small picture used as a symbol for a company or product. Logos are widely used in advertising

macro

A macro is a small piece of software produced by the user in an application. Macros can easily be produced by recording a sequence of actions

margin

Spaces left around a document on the top, bottom, left and right edges of the paper

megabyte

One million bytes

memo

A document which is a short note or message sent from one person to another in a business setting.

memory

Integrated circuits used to store *data*

menu
> A set of options displayed on the screen for the user to choose from

micro-processor
> A complex *integrated circuit* which can recognise and carry out *software* instructions

minutes
> A document which is a record of what happened in a meeting

monochrome
> A screen display with only two colours, usually black and white

motherboard
> A large card which carries the main components of a computer, such as a *micro-processor* and *memory* chips. *Interface cards* are connected to the motherboard

newsletter
> A document usually having one or two pages which summarises recent events. Like a small newspaper, it is often produced for a small group of people

numerical/numeric
> To do with numbers

operating system
> A large and complex piece of *system software* which controls the overall operation of a computer system

order
> A document sent by a customer to a company requesting some goods or services

packing note
> A document sent with some goods listing what has been delivered

page orientation
> Which way round the paper is. Sideways is landscape, 'normal' is portrait

page size
> How big the paper is – A4, A3 and so on

pathnames
> A pathname gives the location of a file, by saying which drive it is on, in which *folder* and so on

PC
> A personal computer – a computer of a size which make sit suitable for one person to use it. A desk-top computer

pixel
> A picture element. One of the dots making up a computer graphic

primary key

> See *key*

PSU

> Power supply unit. The *hardware* component which uses mains electricity and produces voltages suitable to power the other components

query

> In a database, a query searches and selects out the required rows and columns from a table

RAM

> A type of *memory* where the data can be changed, in contrast with *ROM*

readability check

> A common *tool* in a word processor used to check how easy some text is to read

records

> In a *database*, a record is one row in a *table*

refresh rate

> How many times per second a *screen display* is re-drawn

relational database

> A *database* containing data stored in tables with links (relationships) between them

relative reference

> A spreadsheet *cell reference* which gives a cell position as so many rows across and columns down. If the cell is copied elsewhere, the relative reference will refer to a different cell. This is the opposite of an *absolute reference*

report

> In a database, a report is a well-formatted print out of a table or the results of a query. A business report is a formal document reporting the findings of an investigation

resolution

> How sharp a picture is, or how much detail can be seen. This applies to screen displays and printers

ROM

> Read-only memory, a type of *memory* where the data cannot be changed. The opposite of *RAM*

screen display

> A display on a *VDU*

search engine

> On the Internet a search engine is used to find information

secondary key

> See *key*

security

Protecting data from accidental loss or intentional 'hacking'

serif

A little mark at the edges of letters in some fonts. Fonts with serifs are said to be clearer to read

software

Programs. Software is a set of instructions to the computer. The opposite of *hardware*

sort

Put into increasing or decreasing order

specification

A definite check-list of what a computer should have in the way of memory, drives and so on, or a similar definite list of what a system should do

spell checker

A software *tool* which uses a dictionary to check the spelling of words

spreadsheet

An *application* which handles data in the form of a grid with rows and columns, especially for calculations

superscript and subscript

Two ways of formatting characters. Superscripts are towards the top of normal letters, as in 2nd. Subscripts are towards the bottom, as in H_2O

system software

Software which makes the computer work – in contrast with *application* software

table (row and column)

A way of structuring data in the form of rows and columns. The columns go up, and the rows go across. Used in spreadsheets, word processing and database, but in different ways

table of contents

In a book the table of contents lists the items in the book in page number order. This contrasts with the *index* which is in alphabetical order

tags

In *HTML*, a tag is a piece of coding which marks links and formatting

template

A *document* which can be used as a starting point or model for others. Templates are used for spreadsheets and word processing

terabyte

A million million *bytes*

text data type

A *data type* made of letters and other characters

text justification

See *justification*

thesaurus

A *tool* which lists other words with the same or similar meaning

tool

A piece of *software* which does something useful, like a *spelling check* or a *thesaurus*

toolbar

In a GUI, a toolbar is window containing buttons that do related tasks – such as a drawing toolbar

VDU

A visual display unit, sometimes called a monitor

video card

An *interface card* which connects the computer to a *VDU*

virus

A small piece of *software* which tries to hide itself, copy itself and damage a computer system

volatility

Whether *memory* loses its data when power is removed

Web page

A single *HTML document*

Web site

A set of related and linked *web pages*, usually 'owned' by the same person or company

what-if query

In a *spreadsheet*, this means changing the value of one quantity to see what effect that would have

wizard

A piece of software which helps users to do something by asking them a series of questions, then doing the task for them in accordance with what they want

Index

Page references in *italics* indicate tables or diagrams